A NATURAL
HISTORY OF
ZEBRAS

Other books illustrated by UGO MOCHI

A NATURAL HISTORY OF GIRAFFES

Text by DORCAS MacCLINTOCK

HOOFED MAMMALS OF THE WORLD

Text by T. DONALD CARTER

A VOICE FOR WILDLIFE

Text by VICTOR B. SCHEFFER

A NATURAL HISTORY OF ZEBRAS

pictures by UGO MOCHI

text by DORCAS MacCLINTOCK

CHARLES SCRIBNER'S SONS / NEW YORK

Library of Congress Cataloging in Publication Data
MacClintock, Dorcas.
 A natural history of zebras.

 Bibliography: p. 129
 Includes index.
 SUMMARY: Discusses the evolution, relatives, habits,
behavior, habitats, and enemies of zebras.
 1. Zebras—Juvenile literature. [1. Zebras]
I. Mochi, Ugo, 1889-   II. Title.
QL737.U62M3   599'.725   76-12630
ISBN 0-684-14621-5

1 3 5 7 9 11 13 15 17 19 V/C 20 18 16 14 12 10 8 6 4 2

PRINTED IN THE UNITED STATES OF AMERICA

To Paul Bransom

who captures the character and
action of animals in art

Contents

CONTENTS

Preface

FOR Ugo Mochi, an artist who works in black and white and prefers hoofed mammals to all others, zebras are an obvious choice. These striped equids also combine the author's obsession with horses and her love for Africa and its animals.

Each zebra in this book is a cutout, or graphic sculpture, created from a single sheet of paper. Ugo Mochi uses a rough pencil sketch placed over heavy paper (black if the zebra is to be in outline or white if its stripe pattern is to be shown, in which case the finished cutout overlies black paper). He then proceeds with utmost skill, agile fingers, and a small lithographer's knife to cut the animal. As a sculptor, Mochi concentrates on the zebra's form. Zebras in action, zebras in repose, all have that essential quality called character, born of the artist's sure knowledge of zebra forms, gestures, and behavior.

To our families who endured an intrusion of zebras and always encouraged us we give special thanks: Edna Mochi, wife of the artist; my husband, Copeland MacClintock; my parents, Helen and James T. Eason. My daughters Pamela and Margaret, with their pony and horse, taught me much about zebra relatives. Thanks also go to Dr. and Mrs. T. Eric Reynolds of Piedmont, California, with whom I saw zebras in Africa; to Dr. Paul O. McGrew of the University of Wyoming, who introduced me to the study of fossil horses and their teeth; to Dr. B. Elizabeth Horner of Smith College for information about zebras; and to Dr. Friderun Ankel-Simons of Yale University, who read to me from the German. Dr. Harmon C. Leonard and Dr. John J. Wright, veterinarians in Cheshire, Connecticut, were most helpful on aspects of diseases and equid anatomy. Dr. Hans Klingel of the University of Braunschweig supplied photographs of his work with zebras. Peter J. Gogan, graduate student at the University of California, Berkeley, wrote from South West Africa about field studies in progress. James G. Doherty, curator of mammals at the New York Zoological Park, kindly read the manuscript and provided useful comments. I am grateful to Jacqueline Schonewald of the California Academy of Sciences for assistance in reading proof. Again I have been fortunate in having access to the library facilities of Yale University, particularly the Kline Science Library.

DORCAS MACCLINTOCK

A NATURAL
HISTORY OF
ZEBRAS

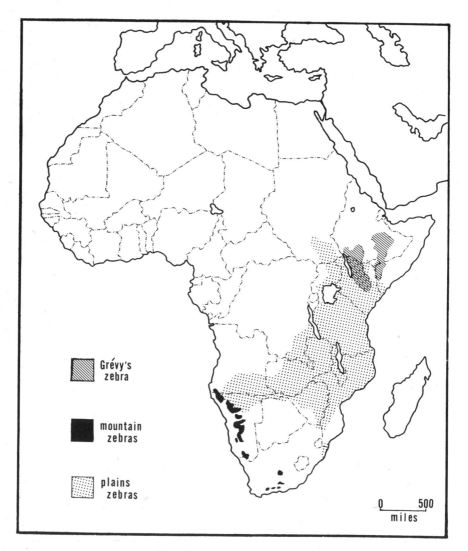

MAP OF AFRICA

showing present-day distribution of the three species of zebras

1. Zebras Today

DUST hovered over the wooded hills and stretches of rich and golden grass of the Mara in southern Kenya. Everywhere I looked vast herds of dark-bodied, humpbacked wildebeests dotted the landscape. With them were small, widely scattered herds of zebras. It was October, late in the dry season. Clouds swelling on the horizon signaled the coming change from dry to wet season. Soon these gathering herds would start their long trek back to the Serengeti.

The zebras I watched were plains zebras, one of three kinds of boldly striped wild horses that live in Africa, a land of dramatic contrasts. Dry, hot, desert-fringe areas of the northeast are habitat for the large, narrow-striped Grévy's zebra, while in the south the smaller mountain zebras are found among hills and mountain ranges.

The name zebra may have come from an Amharic or ancient

PLAINS ZEBRA

GRÉVY'S ZEBRA

Semitic word *zĭgra* (and its derivatives *zĭgora* and *zĭbra*), a word for guinea fowl which originally meant "of a striped black and white color." Or zebra may have come from the Hebrew *tzĕbi*, meaning "splendor" or "beauty."

TARPAN

MOUNTAIN ZEBRA

Zebras, horses, and asses belong to the family Equidae. Living equids are so closely related and fundamentally alike that they are placed in a single genus *Equus*. The tarpan (or European wild horse), Przewalski's horse (or Mongolian wild horse), and domestic breeds,

PRZEWALSKI'S HORSE

SHETLAND   SHIRE

from diminutive Shetland to ponderous Shire, are the zebras' horse relatives. Their wild ass relatives include the large, horselike Asiatic wild
asses or hemiones (kiang, onager, kulan, and khur) and the small,

KIANG

ONAGER

donkeylike African wild asses. The Somali wild ass, still found in parts of Ethiopia, has banded legs and a social organization similar to that of one of the zebras.

Zebras and their relatives belong to a once varied, abundant, and widespread order of mammals, the Perissodactyla. There are three living

KULAN

NUBIAN WILD ASS

families of these odd-toed hoofed mammals: horses and their relatives, the family Equidae; tapirs; and rhinoceroses. Paleotheres, titanotheres, and chalicotheres are extinct perissodactyl groups. All perissodactyls are mesaxonic; that is, the main weight-bearing axis of each foot passes through the middle toe (or third of the ancestral set of five toes), which is always the longest.

In time, as perissodactyls gained speed by running on toe-tips, their

SOMALI WILD ASS

BLACK RHINOCEROSES

lateral toes were reduced to three, or one. First to disappear were "thumb" and "big toe," followed by "little toe." Modern-day tapirs, long-snouted inhabitants of humid forests in South America and Asia, are at this stage of limb modification. With persistent "little fingers," they are four toed in front and three toed behind. Both horses and rhinoceroses developed a three-toed foot. But only the equids carried this trend to the extreme of a one-toed foot.

TAPIR AND YOUNG

2. In the Fossil Record

ZEBRAS trace their family line back in geologic time more than 60 million years to a primitive order of five-toed extinct ungulates called condylarths. These Paleocene herbivores or plant eaters are ancestral to most if not all of the hoofed mammals. Early condylarths had carnivore features that suggest a common origin for carnivores and ungulates, while later condylarths evolved in the direction of hoofed mammals. *Phenacodus*, and presumably the ancestors of the equids, were more dog- than horselike in appearance, but each of their five toes carried a small hoof.

North America was the center of equid evolution. Early equids radiated out from the area that is now the Great Plains and migrated between North America and Eurasia when wide land connections existed during the Cenozoic Era. Although short-lived side branches developed in Eurasia, the main evolutionary line of horses and zebras flourished in North America.

Eocene rocks in Wyoming, New Mexico, Colorado, and Utah contain remains of *Hyracotherium* or eohippus, the "dawn horse." Often it is only a tooth, preserved because of its hard enamel, or a jaw fragment, or a limb bone that is recovered. But from such finds paleontologists are able to reconstruct the whole animal and infer much about its habitat and way of life.

Eohippus stood only 2.2 to 5 hands at the shoulders. (In horse terminology a hand equals 4 inches, roughly the width of a human hand, and is the usual expression of height measurement.) Presumably spotted, this small browsing bush dweller may have looked more like a baby tapir than a horse.

Toe reduction had begun. Eohippus's spreading feet, four-toed in front and three-toed behind, were well suited for running and bounding over soft, humus-covered tropical forest floors.

Eohippus had the full primitive-mammal count of forty-four teeth.

A slight diastema or gap on either side of upper and lower jaws suggests the beginning of a double dental apparatus: front teeth for cropping and back teeth for crushing (and in later forms for grinding). Its low-crowned or brachydont cheek teeth were suited to a browser's diet of leaves and other soft plant foods. Cusps on the molar teeth tend to unite, forming a crested or lophodont pattern. This trend becomes more apparent in later Eocene horses whose premolar teeth are molariform or molarlike.

Size gradually increased. *Mesohippus* of the Oligocene, the first three-toed horse, stood about 6 hands. The outer toe of its front foot was represented by a tiny bony vestige attached to the wrist.

The Miocene brought changes in climate, terrain, and vegetation. As grasslands replaced forests over much of North America, horses

E O H I P P U S   A N D   A N   A R A B I A N   H O R S E

adapted to the role of grass eaters. Their cheek teeth, now a battery of three premolars and three molars, all much alike, on either side of upper and lower jaws, became hypsodont or high crowned, with much of their lengthened crowns retained in bony sockets of skull and jaws. Complicated patterns of enamel mark their grinding surfaces.

Merychippus of the Miocene was larger and longer limbed. It was three toed, but its side toes did not touch ground when it stood. Probably they provided traction in springing and in scrambling over rough ground. Running over hard ground also induced changes. Lateral limb movement, which might cause breaks and strains, became restricted. A grazer, *Merychippus* had a longer neck and widened diastemata that allowed elongation of the skull in front of the eyes without an accompanying increase in number or size of teeth.

The first one-toed horse, pony-sized *Pliohippus*, appeared in the Pliocene. Some primitive forms of *Pliohippus* had tiny side toes; later forms had only vestiges that persisted as long, slender bones beneath the skin.

Equus, the genus of all living horses, asses, and zebras, appeared at the end of the Pliocene, some 3 million years ago. The zebralike early species of *Equus* that wandered over North America usually are considered in a separate subgenus *Equus (Plesippus)*. According to Dr. Paul O. McGrew, a vertebrate paleontologist at the University of Wyoming who has devoted many years to the study of equid evolution, *Equus (Plesippus)* was a zebra and is more appropriately placed in the subgenus *Equus (Hippotigris)* with two of the present-day zebra species. Dr. McGrew maintains that zebras originated in North America, their lineage stemming almost imperceptibly from *Pliohippus*. During the early Pleistocene zebras migrated across the Bering land bridge, through Eurasia, and into Africa. Subsequently they became extinct except in Africa.

Vertebrate paleontologist David P. Willoughby of the Los Angeles County Museum also believes zebras first appeared in North America. Osteometric or bone-measurement data he has collected from the fossil "horses" of the late Pleistocene Rancho La Brea tar pits suggest that these equids may have been giant zebras rather than horses. Willoughby concluded from comparison of bone measurements that "there is good evidence that the present-day species known as Grévy's zebra may have evolved from the Pliocene form *Plesippus*."

Even the quagga, a recently extinct zebra of southern Africa, may have been represented in North America. Measurements of skull and limb bones and skeletal proportions of *Equus occidentalis* led Willoughby to infer a close relationship to the quagga. Carbon 14 datings indicate that this quaggalike equid roamed the grassy plains of what is now southern California some 13,000 to 16,000 years ago.

Another North American Pliocene horse *Equus* (*Astrohippus*) is presumed to have migrated to Eurasia where it gave rise to the true horses *Equus* (*Equus*). These horses reversed the usual route and migrated into North America in mid-Pleistocene.

With a distribution that was worldwide except for Australia, *Equus* flourished during the Pleistocene. Then, some 8,000 years ago near the end of the Pleistocene, horses died out in North America. Their disappearance was part of a large-scale, catastrophic extinction, presumably caused by Paleoindian hunters, that saw a remarkable number of large mammals vanish from the North American scene. In Europe and Asia wild horses lived on, and in Africa zebras thrived, adapting to their Pleistocene environment and its different habitats.

3. A Look at the Zebra

THE zebra's superb design evolved through time as its ancestors adapted to changing environments and responded to constant predator pressure. Specialization of legs, eyes, and teeth fit the zebra for a life of roaming and galloping over hard-soiled plains, eluding predators, and grazing.

A zebra almost always appears in good condition. This is because an extensive layer of fat, the panniculus adiposus, pads its body contours. Underneath its well-rounded shape and hard-bodied equid form is a skeleton basically similar to your own, except for differences in shape, length, and angulation of the bones, and the fact that much more of a zebra's body weight is supported by its forelegs than by its hindlegs. This forward position of its center of gravity is an adaptation for speed.

LIMBS

The most obvious difference between the zebra's skeleton and your own is in limb structure, for the zebra has dispensed with fingers and toes. A galloping, cursorial animal, it stands entirely on the tip of the third digit of each foot, the equivalent of your middle or longest finger and your middle or third toe. The third digit's original nail or claw is expanded as a horny shell or hoof.

While your limbs are flexible, the zebra's more powerful legs have hingelike joints that restrict motion almost entirely to a backward-and-forward plane. Upper limb bones (humerus of forelimb and femur of hindlimb) are contained in the zebra's body, so that the foreleg leaves the body at the elbow, the hindleg at the stifle or true knee. Fusion of lower limb bones (ulna to radius in forelimb and fibula to tibia in hindlimb) further restricts lateral movement.

The zebra's "knee" is actually its wrist or carpus, composed of seven or eight small bones. Six, or sometimes seven, bones form the

14

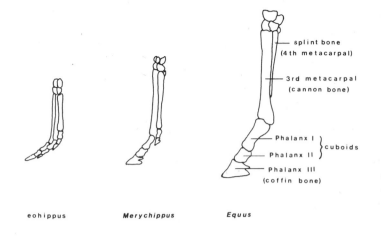

splint bone
(4th metacarpal)

3rd metacarpal
(cannon bone)

Phalanx I }
                } cuboids
Phalanx II }

Phalanx III
(coffin bone)

eohippus   Merychippus   Equus

zebra's hock which corresponds to your ankle or tarsus. Below knee and
hock is a single enlarged metapodial or cannon bone (metacarpal of
forelimb and metatarsal of hindlimb), which corresponds to the third
bone of your palm or instep. Metacarpal length gives the zebra longer
forelegs than any other equid and allies it with the early one-toed
horses.

   Knees and hocks and the four cannon bones form long limb segments that stand perpendicular to the ground. The fetlock joint is supported in a sling or cradle of tendons and ligaments. Two cuboids (Phalanges I and II of the third digit) form the pastern which, when the
zebra stands, slopes forward and downward from the fetlock joint at an
angle of about 155 degrees.

   The terminal segment (Phalanx III) of the third digit is expanded as
the coffin bone that carries the blackish-gray hoof. Like the
hoof, the coffin bone is wider in the weight-bearing forefeet. A shuttle-
shaped sesamoid bone, the navicular, is suspended in the deep flexor
tendon just behind the coffin bone. Two small, pyramidal sesamoids,
situated at the back of the fetlock joint and covered by cartilage, form a
smooth groove or pulley for the same flexor tendon. These three pulley-
like sesamoids, plus another sesamoid, the patella or kneecap, and the
hock act to prevent collapse through overextension of the hinge-type
joints in the zebra's hindlimbs.

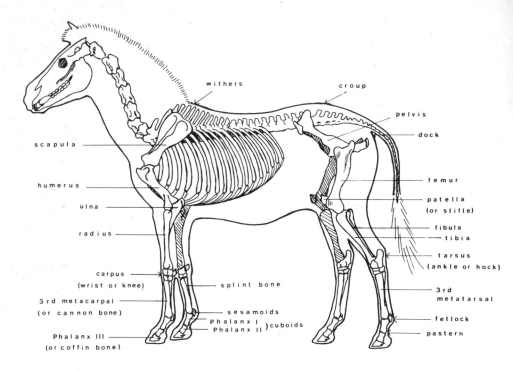

withers   croup

pelvis

dock

scapula

femur

humerus

patella
(or stifle)

ulna

fibula
tibia

radius

tarsus
(ankle or hock)

carpus
(wrist or knee)   splint bone

3rd
metatarsal

3rd metacarpal
(or cannon bone)   sesamoids
Phalanx I)cuboids
Phalanx II

fetlock

Phalanx III   pastern
(or coffin bone)

ZEBRA SKELETON

Differences in limb musculature accompany these skeletal modifications. In contrast to your long, thin limb muscles, the zebra's powerful running muscles are short, fat, and bunched high on its limbs. Most
of them are flexors or extensors whose rubber-band-like actions flex (pull
backward) or extend (straighten) limb segments. For more power in a
fore-and-aft plane, the flexors are grouped on the back of the upper limb
segments and the extensors on the front. Their actions are transmitted
by strong elastic extensions or tendons to the feet. This arrangement of
tendons allows the zebra's legs to remain about the thickness of your
wrist and reduces the weight that must be lifted in walking, trotting, and
galloping.

The zebra's foot is moved by three tendons. An extensor tendon straightens or pulls forward the limb segments; one flexor tendon pulls backward the coffin bone and hoof; another functions to flex the foot at the fetlock (see diagram on page 85).

Muscle fibers have nearly disappeared from one of the zebra's limb muscles. Referred to as a tendon, the interosseous supports one-third of the hoof load. It functions as an elastic spring ligament and, with the sesamoid ligaments, contributes to the automatic springback action of the hoofs.

A complexity of equid ligaments, tough bands of tissue that connect bones and cartilages, developed with the change of the interosseous muscle into a spring tendon. Ligaments and tendons, stretched at impact (when the hoof touches ground), automatically flex the joints, while contraction of muscles controls, assists, and completes movement of the limb.

This springboard action has been likened to that of a child on a pogo stick by Professor Charles L. Camp and Natasha Smith of the University of California, Berkeley, authorities on digital ligaments of equids. "The harder the impact, the higher the bounce—up to the capacity of the apparatus." They noted the perils associated with the development of these complex ligaments: "Among fossil as well as domesticated horses no part of the body is so liable to become injured and permanently disabled, or to develop periosteal exostoses [bony bumps]."

Other modifications for speed include a deep chest to allow for breathing during exertion and a relatively rigid back, concave from withers (point of shoulders) to croup (point of rump). Pelvic structure causes the croup to vary according to zebra species and habitat. In plains zebras the croup is low and rounded, while Grévy's zebra and mountain zebras, inhabitants of semidesert and rocky country, tend to have higher, more angular croups.

Hoof shape also varies with habitat. Grévy's zebra and plains zebras have hoofs with broad, rounded lower rims. Mountain zebras have high, narrow hoofs for sure footing in rocky, hilly terrain. Hoof size as well as habitat determine the shape of the frog, the horny, elastic, V-shaped, impact-absorbing, and slip-preventing pad at the back of each hoof that is the transformed third digital pad.

EYES

The zebra's best defense lies in its ability to see and to flee. With progressive elongation of the skull equid eyes came to be set high in bone-encircled sockets, a position that enables a grazing zebra to see over the grass tops and watch for predators.

The equid eye is large, bulging, and highly specialized. Vision is binocular, that is, both eyes see at once, but only in a relatively narrow zone directly ahead. And even then the zebra's eyes diverge. Vision is also wide angle, each eye taking in a semicircular sweep so that the zebra sees in back and in front without turning its head or moving its eye. The zebra is especially aware of any object that moves at the periphery of its field of vision. Even in bright sunlight its lateral vision is not impaired. Its pupil, the elliptical opening in the iris that determines the amount of light entering the eye, contracts to a horizontal oblong. It is this extraordinary visual capacity that makes it unwise to come up behind a horse, or a zebra, without speaking softly to let it know you are there. It also accounts for the equid tendency to shy, spook, and startle.

Acute as its vision is, the zebra's eye does not have accommodation or adjustment of focus, as your eye has. Objects at varying distances cannot be brought into sharp focus on the same part of the retina, the eye's sensitive layer of photoreceptors. Nor is there a fovea centralis, the tiny retinal depression that is the site of your most acute vision, although a round spot in the center of the equid retina corresponds with the macula lutea, the yellowish area that surrounds the fovea in your eye. Because near and distant objects are in focus but only on different parts of its retina, the zebra must view them from different angles. This is why strange objects are approached first from one side, then the other. Like most mammals, the zebra probably distinguishes varying degrees of brightness rather than colors.

OTHER SENSES

Although less important than sight, the zebra's sense of smell is keen. Large, mobile nostrils, supported by incomplete rings of cartilage, can be distended to test the wind for scents or for blowing after a burst of speed, when their reddish-pink lining is conspicuous.

Hearing also is sharply developed. Ears, black-banded and lined with white hairs, constantly move forward and back to catch the slightest sound.

Vibrissae or tactile hairs cover the zebra's muzzle. For some reason they are especially long and coarse in the Grévy's zebra. The few vibrissae that grow out above and below the eyes and on cheeks and chin also have a protective function.

TEETH

The zebra raises its long supple neck to watch for predators, bends it to bite at and relieve body itches, and lowers it to graze. Grass, snatched by the zebra's mobile lips, is gripped by curved, chisel-like incisors or nipping teeth and torn free with a jerk or tug of its head. Diastemata provide ample room for the zebra's large tongue to move cropped grass to the back of its mouth for grinding.

On each side of the zebra's upper and lower jaws are six columnar cheek teeth (three premolars and three molars). The lower cheek teeth are narrower and less square than the uppers. Worked by powerful jaw muscles, they are efficient grinders. Grass, ground to a pulp, forms boluses or small balls and then is swallowed.

Tough, silica-containing, and abrasive, grass causes constant wear on zebra teeth. The high-crowned teeth, open-rooted and replaced by

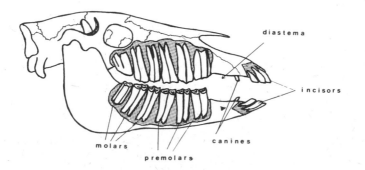

underlying bone as they slowly push up or down out of the jaws to maintain grinding position, grow throughout the zebra's lifespan.

Deciduous or milk teeth precede only incisors and premolars. Wolf teeth, peglike deciduous first premolars, are sometimes retained in the upper jaws, but usually are lost early in life, when permanent premolars fail to replace them. Zebras go through the process of tooth eruption and wear more rapidly than do horses. A zebra is usually a yearling when its first permanent molars erupt, about 2 when the second molars are in place, and about 2½ years old by the time its third molars come into grinding position.

Short, pointed canines or tushes that may have a fighting function usually are developed only in male equids. Thus a zebra stallion has forty teeth while most mares have only thirty-six teeth.

Teeth are made of bonelike dentine, with an outer coating of enamel. In equid cheek teeth this enamel is folded into complex loop patterns, wear-resistant ridges that form a hard grinding surface. Cementum fills and protects the interspaces.

Wear reveals the cheek-tooth patterns of enamel folds that are typical of the three species of zebras, as well as of horses and asses. Wear also causes the gradual obliteration of the dark-stained, enamel-lined cups or infundibula on the flat dentine biting surfaces of the incisors that are useful indicators of equid age. It is doubtful that tooth wear ever is a limiting factor in the lives of wild zebras. But horses that live into their thirties and forties, no longer able to grind their grass, hay, or grain, can be maintained on soft foods.

VESTIGIAL STRUCTURES

Almost all mammals possess anatomical remnants of structures that, in the course of evolution, have lost their function. Paleontologists as well as anatomists have speculated about the purpose of the preorbital pit, a deep depression in front of the eye sockets of *Pliohippus* skulls. Some have regarded the pit as the site of a muscle that moved a flexible, tapirlike nose, which perhaps was an accompanying feature of increasing skull size. Others believe it accommodated a gland. In support of the latter theory is a small, fleshy sac just inside each nostril of living equids. Possibly it is the vestige of a much larger gland that once occupied the preorbital pit.

If ancestral equids did have a preorbital gland, it may have had a function similar to that of the well-developed preorbital glands of some antelopes. With jerking head motions Thomson's gazelles scent-mark their territories, depositing a waxy secretion from their preorbital glands on grass tips.

Chestnuts are flattened, oval, horny structures or callosities, one on the inside of each foreleg, just above the knee. Zebras and asses have only front chestnuts. Other equids have smaller chestnuts on their hindlegs as well. Mountain zebras have the largest chestnuts of any equid, while Grévy's zebra has very small chestnuts. Sometimes regarded as vestigial scent glands, chestnuts may correspond to the "knee brushes" of gazelles and the tarsal glands of deer. When pared they exude a strong-smelling fluid that suggests a onetime glandular function.

More often chestnuts are considered to be vestiges of the first digits and as remnant footpads. Like fingerprints, no two sets of chestnuts are identical. In one case chestnuts were used as thumbprints for positive identification of a stolen horse. A Colorado horse thief was convicted in April 1975 on the evidence of peeled chestnuts, which the horse's owner by chance had retained, matched to the horse's chestnuts.

The ergot is the wartlike spur that projects in a hair tuft on the back, or flexion, surface of each fetlock. Probably it is the vestige of the cushion or pad at the base of the third digit.

Splint bones, much-reduced remnants of the lateral (second and fourth) metapodials, persist with rigid attachment on either side of each cannon bone. Although they may reduce the shock or impact that cannon bones must bear, splint bones often are trouble sites when bony enlargements or "splints" form, sometimes as the result of a kick or blow or from the strain of galloping over hard ground.

MANES AND TAILS

Coarse, upright hairs form the zebra's mane. The fact that biting attacks of fighting zebras often are directed at the mane suggests it has a decoy function, protecting head and neck from serious injury. Manes vary among plains zebras. Southern species have thick manes and forward-curved forelocks, while northern forms have thinner manes and sparse forelocks.

Along the northern limits of their range, in the Karamoja of north-eastern Uganda, in the Sudan, and near the Juba River in Somalia, plains zebras sometimes are maneless. Their naturally hogged manes give them the appearance of small, .striped polo ponies. Occasionally maneless zebras are seen in Kenya and Tanzania; however, it is only in the Karamoja and Juba River areas that maneless zebras are common. In some herds all the adult zebras are maneless; in other herds the mares have manes. Foals always are born with manes. As they reach sexual maturity their manes are shed out and, in the case of maneless zebras, not regrown.

The zebra's relatively long tail, the upper half short-haired and striped and the lower portion a mixture of long black and white hairs, is both an effective fly switch and a useful means of signaling intent. Violent tail switching may express annoyance at the too close approach of another grazing zebra instead of an attempt to get rid of a biting fly.

4. Flying Hoofs and
Barking Calls

ZEBRAS, like other equids, have three gaits: the walk, the trot, and the gallop. The walk is a four-beat gait. Each hoof fall is separate and evenly spaced as legs move forward and back in sequence of left-fore, right-hind, right-fore, left-hind, left-fore, and so on. Trotting is a rapid, two-beat gait. Diagonal leg sets move together to give this sequence of hoof falls: left-fore and right-hind, left-hind and right-fore, left-fore and right-hind, and so on. Twice in each stride (a stride includes all the movements of the legs until they regain the position from which they started and is measured by the distance from one hoofprint to the next hoofprint of the same leg) there is a brief instant when all four hoofs are off the ground.

Galloping is a gait with "leads"; either the left foreleg or the right foreleg leads. With each change of direction a galloping zebra switches leads so that the inside foreleg leads on turns and the body weight is balanced. Galloping on the left lead the hoof-fall sequence is: left-fore, pause, right-hind, double beat of left-hind and right-fore, left-fore, pause. All four hoofs are off the ground once during a stride. At full speed a zebra gallops up to 37 miles an hour.

The zebra's locomotor muscles, more than half of them associated with its hindlimbs, provide powerful driving thrust. At the end of a galloping stride the iliopsoas muscle draws the hindleg forward, flexing it at the hip. Action of the quadriceps muscle causes stifle and hock to extend and the hoof touches ground. Now comes the propelling phase when the caudal or rearmost thigh muscles (biceps, semimembranosus, and semitendinosus) and the large mass of the middle gluteal muscle drive the body forward over the limb. Forequarters and forelimbs absorb the resulting strain and, acting as pivots, convert it into forward motion. The iliopsoas then returns the hindlimb to forward position.

23

A complex series of elastic structures, tendons and ligaments, cooperates to produce the catapulting action of the zebra's limb joints. The fetlock joint bends at an angle of 100 degrees or less as enormous pressure is placed on the hoof; the lower the fetlock joint drops, the greater the stretching force exerted on the flexor tendon. As other legs assume the body weight pressure is reduced and contraction of the spring ligaments rapidly and automatically causes the joint to flex and, aided by flexor muscles whose tendons insert still farther down the toe, helps to propel the body.

The canter is a slowed, three-beat version of the gallop. Theodore Roosevelt and mammalogist Edmund Heller noted in *Life Histories of African Game Animals* that "the gaits of the big zebra [Grévy's] are a slashing trot and a gallop, whereas the small [plains] zebra canters." With a horselike way of going, Grévy's zebra trots with free, high action and its head carried high.

The Scottish geologist Joseph Thomson, who led an expedition through Kenya's Masailand in 1883, described plains zebras "thundering along in great squadrons; here stretching out like racers as they passed in dangerous proximity to the enemy; there massed up at bay with excited mien and head erect, trotting about with splendid action as if daring the hunter to approach."

The mountain zebras' way of going differs from the other zebras'. Alarm causes a herd to gallop toward hilly ground. Unlike plains zebras they do not pause to look back. With heads high and carried nearly horizontally and necks arched backward, they gallop for a short burst, then settle into a ground-covering trot.

Except for leaping up or down steep riverbanks or across dried-up streambeds called dongas, zebras have few opportunities to jump. A stallion in a zoo, startled by a falling branch, is reported to have negotiated a 58-inch fence from a standing start. The record high jump was made by a mountain zebra that cleared the 6-foot wall of a small stone kraal "without touching the top."

When zebras flee, their excited barking calls maintain and reestablish contact between group members, a form of communication that is especially important when herds are pursued by predators at night. Wrote American biologist George B. Schaller, "I particularly liked hearing zebra bray at night, their wild and haunting calls filling the void between stars and earth."

The plains zebra's barking whinny, its contact call, usually is described as beginning with a whistling intake of breath, quickly followed by a succession of calls *kwa-ha! kwa-ha! kwa-ha-ha-ha!* The British artist John Guille Millais, who traveled over the South African veld in the early 1890s, analyzed their call as "a cross between the bellowing of a jackass and the hoarse bark of an aged collie dog." Awakened before sunrise by distant barking, he left his bed beneath a wagon to find a zebra herd some 500 yards away.

According to Heller, the call of Grévy's zebra is "a series of deep grunts interrupted by a whistle-like squeal," very different from the "sharp barking *kwa-ha* of the plains zebras."

Fright is registered by a loud snort, sometimes accompanied by the stamping of a foreleg. Actually there are two alarm calls, a snort much like that of other hoofed mammals and a hoarse call produced by breathing in and out with mouth open. When alarm is signaled, zebras often group in a semicircle. Their alert stances and intent stares transmit a warning to other prey species.

A zebra's alarm snort may cause a lurking or stalking predator, aware its presence has been detected, to give up the hunt. This was observed by American zoologist Richard D. Estes who watched two lionesses in ambush: "Several times one or the other tensed for a spring when a member of the file came slightly closer than the rest. But still they watched until a zebra finally spotted them and snorted in alarm. After the initial bolt, the herd formed up in a half-circle and stood staring at the lionesses. . . . The cats then relaxed, sat up and looked away with bored expressions."

Among the other sounds made by zebras is the loose-lipped blowing, often heard in a grazing herd, that registers contentment and well-being. Short high-pitched squeals of fear and pain sound when zebras fight. A zebra foal's distress squeal brings both mare and stallion to the rescue and alarms the rest of the herd as well.

5. Stripes and Stripe Patterns

EXCEPT for white areas on belly, insides of legs, and crease of well-rounded buttocks, black (or dark brown) and white stripes alternate over the zebra's body with such geometric equality that, wrote the eighteenth-century French naturalist Georges Louis Leclerc Comte de Buffon, "one might almost imagine the rule and compass to have been employed in their distribution."

As to how the zebra got its stripes there is no better account than Rudyard Kipling's. One of his *Just So Stories* tells how spots and stripes developed on leopard, giraffe, and zebra, all of them once " 'sclusively sandy-yellowish-brownish all over." As Kipling tells it, "This was very bad for the Giraffe and the Zebra" for the leopard would lie down by a

" 'sclusively yellowish-greyish-brownish stone or clump of grass, and when the Giraffe or the Zebra . . . came by he would surprise them out of their jumpsome lives." In time and "bit by bit" giraffe and zebra left the High Veldt. "They scuttled for days and days till they came to a great forest, 'sclusively full of trees and bushes and stripy, speckly, patchy-blatchy shadows . . . and after another long time, what with standing half in the shade and half out of it, and what with the slippery-slidy shadows of the trees falling on them, the Giraffe grew blotchy, and the Zebra grew stripy. . . . "

Then comes the often asked question: are zebras white with black stripes or black with white stripes? Usually they are thought of as having black stripes on a white background. However, in 1909 British zoologist Reginald I. Pocock published a paper "On the Colours of Horses, Zebras, and Tapirs" in which he argued that dark-colored ancestral horses had white or yellowish flecks so distributed over their bodies that in the course of evolution they tended to coalesce into longitudinal streaks, much like the markings of a baby tapir. Still later, according to Pocock, these flecks regrouped to form whitish transverse bars or stripes over neck and body. As the white stripes increased in extent they fused, "swamping the dark interspaces," so that all that remains of the zebra's original coat color is the dark spinal line and stripes.

Actually it appears that spotting and striping did precede solid colors. The Grévy's zebra's narrow stripes are regarded as the most primitive coat pattern among living equids. Presumably the mountain zebras' stripe pattern evolved from that of Grévy's zebra, with expansion of the dark stripes on the hindquarters and development of the conspicuous "gridiron" on the croup. Plains zebras exhibit still further progressive stages in stripe reduction. The partly striped quagga, with its chestnut-red body color, may have represented a first step toward the solid coloration of asses, hemiones, and wild horses. The dark spinal stripe, transverse shoulder stripe, and leg bands frequently developed on these zebra relatives suggest a striped ancestry.

Shadow stripes are vestiges of a zebra's once narrow striping. These somewhat less distinct stripes mark the interspaces on hindquarters, flanks, and sometimes even neck of southern races of plains zebras. Occasionally they are seen on northern plains zebras. In 1957 German zoologist Eberhard Trumler reported the unusual occurrence of shadow stripes on a Hartmann's mountain zebra. Captured in Angola and photographed in Portugal's Lisbon zoo, this zebra had well-defined shadow stripes on its hindquarters, which again suggest the mountain zebras' intermediate position between Grévy's zebra and the plains zebras-quagga group in stripe pattern evolution.

Not only does each of the three zebra species have a characteristic stripe pattern but stripes vary from zebra to zebra within a species. This fact undoubtedly facilitates interspecific recognition (where species ranges overlap) as well as intraspecific recognition (among herd members). It also has proved a useful tool in field studies. Stripe patterns, as unique as human fingerprints, can be used for photo-identification. Working in Nairobi National Park Kenyan biologist J. C. Briand Petersen devised a system for photo-file recognition of zebra family stallions. His formula for each zebra is based on lateral stripe configuration, whether or not lateral and scapular (shoulder) stripes are connected, and the number of scapular stripes that are closed or open.

It is hard to imagine a concealing function for the zebra's bold stripe patterns. Nevertheless, the American artist-naturalist Abbott H. Thayer, whose ideas on concealing coloration were elaborated in 1909 by his son Gerald H. Thayer, maintained that zebra stripes "cut their wearers all to pieces and look exactly like the stripings of the lighted reeds across their shadowed background." The younger Thayer even placed cardboard zebras among reeds and grasses to support this theory— as well as somewhat less convincing photographs by the German explorer-naturalist Carl G. Schillings. Among tall reeds that fringe water holes, Thayer contended, stripes obliterate a zebra's outline. The dark body stripes appear as upward extensions of the grasses and the light interspaces as downward continuations of the sky, or so argued Mr. Thayer. Captain Frederick J. D. Lugard (later Lord Lugard), a British soldier and explorer, was another who attributed a concealing function to stripes: "The flickering lights in a forest, and the glancing sunbeams and shadows, are counterfeited exactly by the zebra's stripes."

Much of the time, concealing coloration is of doubtful value among social animals like zebras, whose nervous behavior probably relates to the fact their stripes are conspicuous. Instead of freezing when alarmed, as do most animals whose markings blend with their surroundings, zebras bolt away. It seems obvious that their survival depends on alertness, speed, and the protection that comes from herd formation.

Theodore Roosevelt, naturalist, big-game hunter, and twenty-sixth president of the United States, noted that the zebra's stripes were "highly advertising, when close at hand" and that typically the zebra is "a beast of the open plains." Any possible protective function of striping must be considered in relation to zebra predators; to behavior of predators and prey and the ranges at which attack and flight occur; and to the environment and time of day or night in which the predator-prey encounters usually take place.

In the open, at a distance, stripes blend and zebras appear entirely dark or entirely light, depending upon the light intensity. The narrower stripes of Grévy's zebra merge at somewhat closer range than do the broad stripes of plains zebras. In midday when the sun burns down, heat waves shimmer as they rise from the baked ground, lifting up layers of grassland and creating vast watery mirages. The air oscillates and stripes of distant zebras vibrate. But it is at dawn or dusk or by moonlight, times when zebras are most vulnerable to lions and hyenas, that their stripes merge to a gray that makes their body outlines less visible than the black hulks of their wildebeest companions.

Dark stripes, wide above and tapering below, conceal the zebra by countershading. This form of natural deception eliminates the effects of three-dimensional lighting and causes loss of the normal visual clues by means of which a zebra is recognizable. When Kipling's leopard jumped the zebra "in the starlight that fell all stripy through the branches" he could not see his prey, although it "smelt like Zebra, and . . . felt like Zebra, and . . . kicked like Zebra." So the leopard sat on the zebra's head (a standard technique to keep any equid down) until morning. When daylight revealed the zebra's stripes, the leopard asked: "What in the world have you been doing to yourself, Zebra? . . . You haven't any form." Thus the leopard noted that sharply contrasting stripes break up the zebra's body outline and destroy its appearance of solid form.

American zoologists Peter Marler and William J. Hamilton III demonstrated the principle of disruptive margins in *Mechanisms of Animal Behavior* by placing a mountain zebra next to a longitudinally striped "pseudo zebra." Viewed from 10 feet the zebra whose transverse stripes form disruptive edges is invisible, while the pseudo zebra is still readily seen. It has been suggested that transverse striping makes a zebra appear larger than it actually is, a factor that might cause a lion to miscalculate when it leaps. However, it must be noted that lions rarely leap at their prey and that most of their hunting is done at night when zebra stripes have lost their contrast.

In 1912 Sir Richard Lydekker, a British naturalist, observed: "At a distance less than that at which the whole of the stripes melt into a confused blur, the general effect is to render the animal much less conspicuous than would be the case if the stripes were of the same width throughout, and took the same direction on all parts of the skin." Thus he noted the optical disruption caused by stripes that are vertical in front and obliquely patterned on the hindquarters of Grévy's zebra and mountain zebras. A plains zebra's pronounced midbreak in stripe direction, marked by its characteristic Y-shaped saddle, divides its body into anterior and posterior halves and produces the optical illusion of two

distinct objects. Stripe width also causes disruption of form. Broadly striped flanks that make a zebra appear nearer than the narrower striped portions of its body, or cause confusion about the direction in which a zebra is moving, occasionally may deceive a predator. Wide neck stripes disrupt the fine stripes on a Grévy's zebra's head and shoulders. Stripe direction and stripe width combine to divide a plains zebra into four blocks: head, neck, shoulders and forepart of body, and flanks and hindquarters.

Stripe patterns can be deceptive in herd situations, when zebras are tightly bunched. Ambush at a water hole results in a sudden confusion of stripes. In the blur of wheeling, plunging forms individual zebras are almost impossible to distinguish.

Zebras seldom seek shade. The fact that their black stripes absorb slightly more heat from the sun's rays than do their white reflective interspaces suggests striping may have a temperature-regulating, venetian-blind function. Dense and short, the hairs of a zebra's coat prevent the sun's rays from penetrating to the skin. Shininess reflects more than half of the heat from solar radiation. Possibly the narrow and numerous stripes that make the Grévy's zebra appear almost gray are added protection in a hot, dry habitat.

Leg bands are well defined in Grévy's zebra and mountain zebras; plains zebras' legs also are banded to the hoofs in northern subspecies, but only to, or just below, knee and hock in southern races.

From the forelock narrow facial stripes diverge widely between the eyes, converge over the nose, and, except in Grévy's zebra which has a conspicuous white noseband, connect with the velvety blackish-gray muzzle.

Melanism, erythrism, and albinism, tendencies to black, red, and white pigmentation, influence coat color in all mammals. Northern plains zebras are black-striped; southern subspecies have brown stripes. The reddish-brown striping of Grévy's zebra reveals an erythristic trend.

Now and then a plains zebra appears more black than white because it has a reverse stripe pattern. As in a photographic negative, its white interspaces appear black and its dark stripes white. Occasionally a zebra's body stripes run together to form a mottled pattern, or it is so melanistic that it appears merely flecked with white.

In 1911 a subspecies of plains zebra was named for a game ranger, G. H. Goldfinch, who spotted a herd near Nakuru, Kenya, in which all the zebras were marked by a large white patch in the middle of their backs. Apparently the back patches were a short-lived mutation, for the subspecies is no longer valid.

An albinistic Grévy's zebra mare, shot in 1906 by Kenya game warden A. Blayney Percival and mounted in the British Museum (Natural History), had faint cream-colored stripes and, according to Percival, light-colored eyes. South Africa's Tring Museum claims an almost white plains zebra in its collection.

Environment also influences zebra coloration. Near Lake Magadi in Kenya, a barren area of soda flats and scrub vegetation, plains zebras are brown striped and their wildebeest companions are sandy hued.

6. Grévy's Zebra

THIS was the striped horse exhibited in Rome by Caracalla, the fierce and aggressive emperor who was named for the long cloak or *caracallus* he made popular. During his 211–217 A.D. reign Caracalla, whose real name was Marcus Aurelius Antoninus, lavished money on completing the vast public baths and on the circuses. There were several circuses in Rome. On public holidays thousands of Roman citizens flocked to the long, narrow arenas and filled tiers of stone benches to watch chariot races, gladiatorial combats, and parades of wild animals. When the procession of

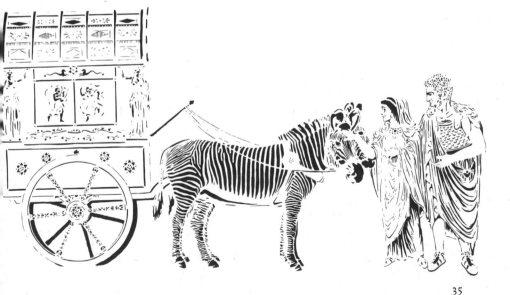

wild animals entered the arena the zebras often were led with halters and lead shanks. On special occasions, when the emperor was present, they were harnessed to an elaborately decorated cart. Caracalla was indeed proud of his zebras.

In spite of its association with ancient Rome, this striped equid was the last of the zebra species to gain scientific recognition. In 1882 Menelik II, king of Shoa and emperor of Abyssinia, sent a live zebra as a gift to Jules Grévy, president of the French Republic. After a short time in the Jardin des Plantes zoo the animal died. Its skin was mounted by taxidermists in the Natural History Museum in Paris.

Shortly after the zebra was placed on exhibit, French zoologist Alphonse Milne-Edwards noticed differences in the stripe pattern that indicated it was not, as had been supposed, a mountain zebra. He named the new species in honor of the French president and sent photographs to Mr. Percival L. Sclater who exhibited them at a meeting of the Zoological Society in London. Edward Oustalet, another French zoologist, described the mounted skin which then became the type specimen of Grévy's zebra (*Equus grévyi*).

An account of Grévy's zebras in the wild was supplied by British Army Captain H. G. C. Swayne, who traveled through Somaliland in the early 1890s: "The zebras, of which I saw probably not more than 200 in all, were met with in small droves of about half a dozen on low plateaux covered with scattered thorn bush and glades of 'durr' grass, the soil being powdery and red in colour with an occasional outcrop of rocks."

In a letter dated 1894 the elephant hunter Arthur H. Neumann described a zebra he shot in Kenya: "A beautiful creature he was—a fine young stallion, larger and far handsomer than Burchell's zebra, the stripes much narrower, except one very broad dark one down the back."

Largest of the zebras, the mulelike Grévy's zebra averages 14.1 hands and sometimes stands as tall as 15 hands, the size of a small horse. Stallions weigh between 780 and 950 pounds.

Numerous narrow, close-set vertical stripes cover the Grévy's zebra's powerful body and blend into a barren shortgrass-thick scrub habitat that often is distorted by heat shimmer. The vertical croup stripes are arranged concentrically around the root of the tail. A characteristic triple-arch pattern is formed on each side of the rump where croup stripes, flank stripes, and hindleg stripes meet. A broad spinal stripe, widest along the mid-back, is bordered by white. The belly also is white. Facial stripes stop well short of the brown nose patch and grayish muzzle. The long legs are banded to the hoofs.

A tall, thick, erect mane, once used by Galla tribesmen of the eastern Ethiopian highlands to adorn the necks of their horses, tops the short neck and extends forward between large, rounded, heavily haired ears as well as back onto the withers.

In addition to narrow vertical striping and big rounded ears, both features of forest dwellers, Grévy's zebra exhibits a number of other primitive characters which suggest it has changed little in the last 2 million years: a long-faced appearance due to elongation of muzzle and diastemata, a cheek-tooth pattern little changed since the Pliocene, short neck vertebrae, long scapulae or shoulder blades, and splint bones, vestiges of its lateral metapodials, that are the longest of any equid's.

On the basis of these features Heller proposed in 1912 that Grévy's zebra be placed in a separate genus, *Dolichohippus*. The name was appropriate, for *dolicho* comes from a Greek word meaning "long" and refers to the zebra's body and leg length as well as to its long, narrow head; *hippus*, of course, means "horse." But few scientists favored the change and *Dolichohippus* was relegated to a subgenus, separating

Grévy's zebra from the other zebras, which are grouped in the subgenus *Hippotigris*.

Among the native African names for Grévy's zebra are the Somali *fer'o*, the N'dorobo *kanka*, and the Swahili *kangani*.

Grévy's zebra's range, the northernmost of zebra ranges, is one of semiarid and desert country in northern Kenya and southern Ethiopia, and three isolated parts of Somalia. It extends north to the Lake Zwai region in Ethiopia, east to the coastal fringe of subtropical scrub in Somalia, west to the Lake Rudolf-Rift Valley line, and south as far as the wide and deep Tana River that drains east from the Aberdare-Mount Kenya Highlands.

7. Mountain Zebras

MOUNTAIN ranges and hills from southern Angola along the coastal fringe of South West Africa (Namibia) into South Africa are the habitat of small, narrow-bodied, donkeylike zebras that stand no more than 12 hands at the shoulders. A dewlap, or pendant skin fold on the underside of the neck, is a mountain zebra characteristic. The mane is thick and erect. From croup to withers the hairs of the narrow spinal stripe grow forward rather than backward. The vertical body stripes that connect with the spinal stripe continue back to the tail, but stop cleanly along the flanks so that, except for a ventral stripe, the belly is white. Broad black and white stripes trend horizontally over the hindquarters. A gridiron pattern, another mountain zebra characteristic, is formed by the series of short transverse stripes that connect spinal stripe and uppermost rump stripes. Facial stripes are narrow and brownish; the muzzle is tan. Legs are banded to the narrow, asslike hoofs.

So well adapted to its high-altitude environment is this species that its heart, which must pump blood thickened by high content of oxygen-conveying red corpuscles, weighs approximately three times that of a plains zebra.

The rare Cape mountain zebra (*Equus zebra zebra*) was the first of the striped equids to receive scientific recognition. Smallest of all the zebras, it has black stripes so closely placed that they appear wider than the intervening white spaces.

Once abundant, this sure-footed uplander the Afrikaners called bergkwagga, wildepaard, or dauw ranged from the Namaqualand region of South Africa through the hills and mountains of the Cape Province (or Cape Colony as it then was) to the southern end of the Drakensberg chain. In 1840 William Cornwallis Harris, an Indian army officer turned Nimrod, described mountain zebras in their habitat: "Seeking the wildest and most sequestered spots, the haughty troops are exceedingly difficult to approach, as well on account of their watchful hab-

40

its and extreme agility and fleetness of foot as from the abrupt and
inaccessible nature of their highland abode. Under the special charge
of a sentinel so posted on some adjacent crag as to command a view of
every avenue of approach, the chequered herd whom 'painted skins
adorn,' is to be viewed perambulating some rocky ledge, on which the
rifle ball alone can reach them."

In spite of Dutch laws established as early as 1656 to protect mountain zebras, the rifle balls of Boer hunters did reach them. Farmers and
trekkers blazed away at mountain zebras at the same time they deci-
mated the teeming herds of the veld. According to Harris, during the
1800s a landowner named Mynheer was engaged in mountain zebra
dealing. Regularly he chased herds "from the mountain fastnesses," and
exported them at considerable profit to the Indian Ocean island of
Mauritius where the zebras were trained to harness.

Early naturalists, among them the Swedish botanists Carl Peter
Thunberg and Anders Sparrman, and the English botanist William J.
Burchell, expressed dismay at the apparent disregard of the Dutch

settlers for the natural world around them. In the spring of 1811 Burchell noted: "We passed Paardeberg . . . so named from the Wilde Paard, which at that time inhabited it; . . . at the present day, not one is to be found there." By 1850 the game herds were all but exterminated in South Africa.

The Cape mountain zebra would have become extinct except for the fact that a few Boer families, the Michaus, the Lombaards, and the Heinses, kept a few of these zebras on their farms. In 1937, when a farm near Cradock was bought by the South African government and proclaimed Mountain Zebra National Park, there were only six zebras within its boundaries (five stallions and a mare). By 1950 two aged stallions remained and the Cape mountain zebra was in imminent danger of extinction.

A year later J. K. Lombaard, whose farm adjoined the park, donated his herd of eleven (five stallions and six mares). A fenced corridor was constructed so that these zebras could be moved into the park and a park biologist was appointed to supervise the herd. In 1953 the first foal was born. By 1964 the herd had grown to twenty-five. Through purchase of neighboring farms, 12,700 acres were added to the park and the "Doornhoek herd" of thirty Cape mountain zebras was purchased from the Michau brothers.

Much of the twenty-five square miles of Mountain Zebra National Park is a sweet-veld plateau 4,000 to 6,500 feet above sea level, covered by a variety of grasses and shrubs. Valleys and some of the mountain slopes are wooded. Although eland, white-tailed gnu, gemsbok, blesbok, springbok, mountain reedbuck, and klipspringer share their refuge, the mountain zebras keep to themselves.

In 1965 twenty-five stallions and thirty-three mares were tallied in the Cradock herd. Nine family groups had an average size of 4.5 zebras, while the single bachelor band consisted of six animals. Two years later the zebra population had increased to sixty-nine. Family group size averaged 6.3 zebras; two bachelor bands had eight and four members. Three of the original groups had lost their stallions (one by death, two by capture for zoos). These groups had been taken over as units by other stallions. In one family group the herd stallion's role had been usurped by a former bachelor. A number of young mares had been abducted as fillies by stallions from other groups. By 1969 the zebra population in the national park at Cradock stood at ninety-eight.

Outside the park a few widely scattered remnant herds have been located. Hopefully the scientific management practices and strict protection that saved the Cape mountain zebra from its perilous brush with extinction will continue to improve its chances for survival.

There are records of zebras that once roamed the mountains near Cape Town. Reportedly these animals resembled the Cape mountain zebra in conformation and color but were the size of the larger Hartmann's mountain zebra. Possibly the ranges of the two subspecies overlapped and interbreeding occurred in this area.

Hartmann's mountain zebra (*Equus zebra hartmannae*), with narrower stripes than the Cape mountain zebra and an off-white ground color, ranges from southern Angola south through South West Africa into the northwest corner of South Africa. It is best seen in Etosha National Park, in the Kaokoveld, in mountain ranges and fringes of the Namib Desert, and in a special reserve in the Naukluft, 150 miles south of Windhoek, South West Africa. Elsewhere these zebras lack protection and are shot by hunters and farmers.

Hartmann's mountain zebra numbers have dropped alarmingly, from an estimated 50,000 to 5,000 in the last twenty years. Their existence in the wild is threatened by competition from livestock and by increasing use of gameproof fencing which often stretches for miles, restricting the zebras' normal seasonal movements and sometimes cutting off their access to water. Both Hartmann's mountain zebra and Cape mountain zebra are included in the *Red Data Book* published by the International Union for Conservation of Nature and Natural Resources, a listing of wild animals (and plants) that are in danger of extinction.

In their dry, scrubby, semidesert habitat Hartmann's mountain zebras can go for several days without water. During the rainy season these zebras migrate into canyons of the Namib Desert where their unique water-seeking behavior has earned them the reputation of being the water engineers of the Namib. Sniffing out small pools that lie below the sand and gravel of dry streambeds, the zebras paw two- to three-foot holes to uncover fresh water. Other desert animals also benefit from water holes dug by the zebras.

8. Plains Zebras

THE Burchelline or common zebras are the most numerous and widely distributed of the striped equids, as well as the ones most often seen in zoos and circuses. In spite of a Swahili name, *punda milia*, that means "striped donkey," these zebras have shorter heads and smaller ears and are more ponylike in conformation than their longer-headed and larger-eared zebra relatives. Generally they are referred to as Burchell's zebras; however, to avoid confusing them with the extinct subspecies that is the true Burchell's zebra it seems preferable to call them plains zebras.

An estimated 500,000 of these round-bodied zebras live in savanna (wooded grassland) and plains areas from the southern Sudan to northern South Africa. Except for the fact their numbers are fewer, northern plains zebras are found over much of their original range. Perhaps two-thirds of the total plains zebra population roams the vast Serengeti-Mara region east of Lake Victoria in Tanzania and Kenya, where migrating herds sometimes stretch across the grassland as far as the eye can see. The southernmost plains zebras are represented by isolated populations in South West Africa and in the Zululand district of South Africa. Plains zebras are gone today from the Orange Free State, the Cape, Natal, and Transvaal provinces in South Africa, and Botswana.

Subspecies are intended to designate distinct geographical types. Variation, individual as well as geographic, in stripe patterns caused a proliferation of plains zebra subspecies. Whenever a big-game hunter or explorer bagged a zebra that had an unusual stripe pattern, a new subspecies was named. From the eighteenth century on, naturalists and artists described and illustrated zebras with aberrant patterns, stripes that range from wavy or interrupted bands on flanks and hindquarters to dark, mottled patterns that cover the body. In 1936 Angel Cabrera, a South American mammalogist, attempted to sort out some thirty-five subspecies described between 1788 and 1924. His conclusion that there

45

B Ö H M ' S   Z E B R A

are only four subspecies or geographic races is more or less accepted
by scientists today.

The East African subspecies, Böhm's (and Grant's) zebra (*Equus
burchelli boehmi*), stands about 13.2 hands, the size of a medium pony.
Broad vertical black stripes, seven to ten on the neck and three or four
on the forequarters, give way to backward-trending barrel stripes. Lateral
stripes often join both the spinal stripe and the ventral belly stripe.
Stripes are nearly horizontal on the hindquarters. The range extends from
southern Sudan, Ethiopia, and Somalia south into the Karamoja district
of Uganda and through Kenya and Tanzania as far as the upper Zambezi River.

Grant's zebra, named in honor of the African explorer James

SELOUS'S ZEBRA

Augustus Grant, is an altitudinal variation of this subspecies, found in more upland habitats.

The zebra named for British sportsman Frederick Courtenay Selous (*Equus burchelli selousi*) has more neck stripes (ten to thirteen) and vertical body stripes (four to eight) and its stripes and interspaces are narrower than those of Böhm's zebra. It ranges from the lower Zambezi River south to the Limpopo River in Mozambique, and occurs in eastern Zambia and Malawi.

Shadow stripes are well developed on flanks and hindquarters of the Damaraland (and Chapman's) zebra (*Equus burchelli antiquorum*). Its stripes are not the jet black of northern plains zebras, and its ground color is cream rather than white. From Benguela in Angola this zebra

CHAPMAN'S ZEBRA

ranges through Damaraland in South West Africa and east into the Transvaal and Zululand provinces of South Africa.

A north-south trend in leg striping is apparent in plains zebras. Northern plains zebras (Böhm's zebra and Selous's zebra) have legs that are banded to the hoofs. To the south, Chapman's zebra has incomplete leg bands that reach almost ot its hoofs, while the Damaraland zebra's leg bands extend only to knee and hock. The extinct Burchell's zebra (and the quagga) had no leg markings. This trend in leg striping is accompanied by reduced belly striping.

Dark brown stripes and shadow stripes were so reduced on the hindquarters that, when viewed from behind, a Burchell's zebra appeared white. Its anterior barrel stripes did not join the ventral belly stripe and except for incomplete bands that occasionally marked the hocks, its legs were white. Immense herds of Burchell's zebras, called bontequaggas or bontkwaggas (painted quaggas) by the Boers, once roamed the grasslands from southern Bechuanaland (now Botswana) to the Orange River in South Africa.

In 1811 William J. Burchell set off on a two-year trek into the South African interior. His Cape wagon was equipped with a small reference library of some fifty books. Burchell kept detailed field notes and assembled a large collection of plants, birds, and mammals that in-

D A M A R A L A N D   Z E B R A

cluded specimens of the zebra later to be named *Equus burchelli bur-chelli*.

Burchell's zebras were wantonly slaughtered by the colonists who used their skins to make connecting bands for machinery. Their eventual extermination was part of the demise of southern Africa's wildlife. When a stallion in Vienna's Schönbrunn Zoo died in 1908, a single Burchell's zebra survived, but only for a few years, in the London zoo.

BURCHELL'S ZEBRA

9. Field Studies

MUCH of what is known about zebras comes from extensive field studies made by a husband-and-wife team of German ethologists (animal behaviorists). From 1962 to 1965 Dr. Hans Klingel of Braunschweig University and his biologist wife Ute (pronounced Oota) observed the social behavior of plains zebras in Ngorongoro Crater in Tanzania. They also studied plains zebra populations in the Serengeti National Park in Tanzania, the Wankie National Park in Rhodesia, Kruger National Park in South Africa, and the Etosha Pan area of South West Africa. Dr. Klingel's research focused on the composition and size of zebra groups in these different populations, their social organization, their home ranges, and their reproductive habits.

In 1965 and 1967 the Klingels turned their attention to investigating the family life of mountain zebras. Again they traveled to South West Africa, this time to observe the Hartmann's mountain zebra. Then they went to Cradock, South Africa, to study the Cape mountain zebra.

A year later, in Kenya, the Klingels began a field study of Grévy's zebra that was to reveal a different social structure.

Many of the methods of field study, such as counting, aerial photography, and food-habits investigations, are carried out without actual handling of the animals. When research involves marking, measuring, or instrumenting (attaching a radio-transmitting collar so that the animal can be followed), capture and handling are necessary first steps. The tracking of marked animals reveals much about their way of living.

During the Klingels' two-year study of plains zebras in Ngorongoro Crater 124 animals (most of them herd stallions) were darted using a Palmer Capchur gun, operated by compressed carbon dioxide, or a crossbow. The zebras were immobilized with succinylcholine chloride and, more successfully with a morphine-like drug called M99 (Etorphine). Cropping of tails and manes, branding with letters of the alphabet, and ear tags were used in combination as marking methods. Squared-off tail hairs

51

proved useful as field marks for up to two years. With binoculars the Klingels could read the brand of a "bang-tailed" individual. Ear tags tended to cause infections and to drop off. Numerous and narrow stripes complicated recognition of individual Grévy's zebras, so the Klingels added yellow collars or belly bands to cropping and branding.

The Klingels marked one zebra in a group and then used neck-stripe patterns for recognition of other members in the group. Photographs of both sides of a zebra's neck were put on a file card which was used for field notes on the animal. Photographic recognition, a method other ethologists were to adopt, enabled the Klingels to keep track of some 600 zebras.

Dr. Toni Harthoorn, a veterinarian in Africa who has devoted years to perfecting methods of immobilizing elephants, lions, hyenas, and other wild animals, assisted the Klingels with their first attempts to dart zebras. He recalled the ethologists at work: "Hans would drive a battered Land-Rover which tended to shed springs like autumn leaves, needing constant small repairs which were effected as a matter of course throughout the day. He would spot a known zebra with field glasses and call out a formula [based on neck-stripe pattern] while Ute, with card-index box on her lap, would industriously go through and produce the required card."

At first the Klingels estimated zebra ages by comparison with animals of known ages. Eventually they found they could trace twenty-one different stages of tooth eruption, replacement, and wear. Seven of these stages consisted of only milk teeth; four stages involved both milk and permanent teeth; and ten stages were determined by degrees of wear on permanent teeth.

With the Klingels' day-after-day observations came a growing fondness for the zebras; for, as Dr. Harthoorn has observed, "marking animals and getting to know individuals often creates a deep affection as a bond is established between observer and observed."

B. L. Penzhorn, an ecologist in South Africa, has studied the Cape mountain zebra. An American graduate student, Peter J. Gogan, has turned his zebra research interests from a food-habits investigation in Tanzania to Etosha National Park where the ranges of two species overlap.

The complexity of a large animal's relationship with its environment and other animals is such that no species is studied by itself. For this reason, the observations of field biologists, studying such diverse animals as wildebeests (Richard D. Estes), giraffes (Dieter Backhaus), black rhinoceros (John Goddard), hyenas (Hans Kruuk, Jane Goodall), lions (George B. Schaller), and wild dogs (Wolfdietrich Kuhme, Hugo van Lawick), have contributed to an understanding of some of the ways of zebras. Happily there is much that remains to be learned about these striped equids.

10. Social Organization

PLAINS animals generally are social. Like the zebra, most of them evolved from small, solitary forest dwellers. The correlation between social behavior and open grassland habitat is nowhere more evident than in Africa. Not only are the hoofed animals social, but they are preyed upon by carnivores that also are highly social: lions, hyenas, and wild dogs.

Plains zebras exhibit a social structure that is unique among hoofed mammals. Remarkably stable small groups form the basic social units, held together by personal bonds between individual zebras. Although wanderings are limited by zebras' dependence on water, the groups are nonterritorial, nomadic, and often migratory.

Grazing brings zebra groups together in large herds that sometimes number 5,000 or more individuals. Mingling also occurs at water holes. But these are merely aggregations within which zebra groups maintain their coherence and are quick to sort themselves out when danger threatens. As each family bunches together the stallion places himself between the predator and the mares and foals. Such compartmentalized social organization provides safety for individual zebras in each tight-knit group and differs from the reaction of the zebras' wildebeest grazing companions, which flee with wild plunges and bucks in a mob panic scene. Zebras, as Schaller has observed, "have a steadier personality than wildebeest, less given to energetic mindlessness."

FAMILY GROUPS

A stallion and a few mares (one to six) and their offspring make up these small groups. There may be as many as sixteen, but family-group size averages seven zebras. Although each unit is "owned" by the stallion, the group's cohesion actually comes from bonds that exist between the mares and between the mares and the stallion. This fact makes zebra family groups more stable and more durable than the harem groups formed by male-herding activities of many other hoofed animals. So strong are these ties between mares that when a stallion is killed or driven off, his family group usually is taken over intact by another stallion.

COMMUNICATION

Within the family group mares are highly exclusive. They will have nothing to do with zebras of other groups and are antagonistic toward them. The family stallion, however, seeks out and approaches all other stallions in ritual greeting. Much whinnying back and forth precedes the meeting of two stallions. With extended necks, pricked ears, and partly open mouths, stallions make nose-to-nose contact. Then each shoves his head against the other's flank and sniffs the genital region. Again the stallions smell noses, then rear up on their hind legs in a farewell jump. Greeting between an adult and a submissive young stallion involves only nose sniffing.

As with any animals, communication among zebras depends upon signals and responses. Signals are of two kinds: discrete (those presented in a simple on-or-off way) and graded (the greater the intensity of emotion the more exaggerated and prolonged the signal). Zebras show hostility or threat by laying back their ears, while friendly intent is signaled by upward pointing ears. Both ear positions are discrete signals. Opening of the mouth is a graded signal. Composite facial communication occurs when two signals are combined to convey different meanings. Added to an ear signal, either threat or greeting, the open mouth signifies, according to degree of gape, a zebra's intensity of feeling.

DOMINANCE AMONG FAMILY MEMBERS

A dominance hierarchy exists within the family group. The stallion is dominant, but in moving from place to place the group usually is led by a mare. Generally it is the oldest mare that has the next highest rank and is the group's leader. Other mares follow her in strictly observed order of rank. A mare that moves ahead of her customary place is threatened by bared teeth and rumps turned to kick and quickly resumes her proper place. This rank order may change every few months or may remain constant.

Each mare is accompanied by her offspring in reverse order of dominance, youngest foal first and oldest last. Sometimes a mare is trailed by a suckling, a yearling, and a two-year-old. A young foal occupies a position just one peg below that of its dam, and its position is respected by lower-ranking mares.

The stallion trails behind his family, to defend it against other stallions and to herd straggling mares or foals. Now and again he travels alongside his family, herds the lead mare to change direction, and even takes the lead on treks to water or during migration.

Mares usually stay with their family groups throughout their adult lives. Of the forty-one family groups the Klingels observed in Ngorongoro Crater over a two-year period, twenty-nine remained unchanged. Predators presumably accounted for the adult mares that disappeared from six of the groups. Only one adult mare left her family group to join another. The fact that she returned a few days later suggests the strength of family group bonds.

When a zebra becomes separated it is searched for by the other members of its group. Stallions keep track of their mares and foals. Mares search only for their own fillies and colts. This aspect of group behavior was noted by the Klingels while they were immobilizing zebras. Inadvertently mares, foals, and stallions became separated. On two occasions herd stallions seized the necks of still tranquilized mares with their teeth and led them back to their family groups. The death of a four-year-old stallion, still with his family group, revealed the strength of father-son bonds. The family stallion tried again and again to rouse the young stallion, and later left his mares for six hours, going from group to group, searching and calling for his son.

Stallions are replaced only when they are weakened by sickness or old age, or if they are killed by a predator. Stallions changed in five of the forty-one family groups. Three groups were taken over as units by other stallions on the deaths of the original family stallions. Younger stallions won battles to replace aged stallions in the other two groups. Stallions that are replaced live out the rest of their days in bachelor bands, often joined by colts or young stallions that leave the family group, presumably because of allegiance to their sire.

FILLIES

Usually fillies are abducted by other herd stallions when they are 1½ or 2 years old. Stallions cluster around any herd in which there is an estrous filly, attracted by the conspicuous posture that marks the extent of time she is in heat. During this period the herd stallion vigorously defends the filly, usually his daughter, against repeated attempts of would-be suitors to cut her out from the group. It is apt to be when he pursues one of these stallions for a distance that an opportunist succeeds in abducting her. But, as fights over fillies continue for the duration of their estrous periods, the abductor seldom keeps his filly.

Not until she is 2½ years old does a filly become a permanent member of a group. Even then she first undergoes probation, for the other mares are hostile and greet her with bites and kicks. Eventually she is accepted into the family and her possession by the family stallion is respected by all other zebras. Although her active breeding life began with her first estrus, conception rarely occurs before a filly is 2½ years old.

A Grévy's zebra filly stays with her dam until she is sexually mature, when her estrous stance attracts stallions and causes separation of filly and mare.

COLTS

Sometime between their first and fourth years colts leave their family group to join bachelor bands. Leaving may be precipitated if the arrival of a sibling breaks the bond between mare and colt. Or, if there are no other colts in the family group, a colt will seek and join playmates in a bachelor band. The running, fighting, and greeting games, typical of colts and young stallions at play, are a necessary part of growing up.

Usually a Grévy's zebra colt is at least 3 years old before he leaves his dam. After the mare-foal bond is broken, both colts and fillies come and go among Grévy's zebra herds.

BACHELOR BANDS

Possession of mares by family stallions results in a large surplus of males. A few prefer to lead solitary lives, but most stallions consort in bachelor bands of two to fifteen (usually about three) individuals. Although their composition varies from time to time, these groups are held together by bonds between the stallions. The leader is always an adult stallion. Other adult stallions appear to have equal rank, but an order of dominance is apparent among the younger stallions and colts. Males remain bachelors until their fifth or sixth year.

MOUNTAIN ZEBRAS

Also nonterritorial, mountain zebras range in small, permanent herds that are family groups (a stallion and one to four mares and their foals) or bachelor bands. Some stallions are solitary. Often groups meet, mingle, graze together for a time, then move off. Family stallions lead their mares and foals in single file along mountain paths and head their groups on treks to water. At the water hole a stallion usually stands guard while his mares and foals drink.

Nervous and shy as a result of hunting pressure, Hartmann's mountain zebras are difficult to approach. The Klingels used a blind at a water hole from which they observed zebras coming and going.

TERRITORIALITY AND GRÉVY'S ZEBRA

Instability characterizes the small grazing herds of four to fourteen Grévy's zebras. No permanent bonds exist between any two or more adults of this zebra species. The Klingels observed stallion groups, mare groups, mares-and-foals or nursery groups, and mixed herds and found no indication of a stable order of dominance or leadership among zebras. In fact, the groups are constantly changing as zebras come and go. When an individual leaves a herd it may wander off alone, or be followed by others. Even during migration lead zebras change places without contest. Sometimes groups congregate to form large herds.

Solitary Grévy's zebra stallions often are territorial. Their territo-

riality may represent the original form of social organization among equids, for bush-dwelling, browsing eohippus is presumed to have been territorial, its habits similar to those of the tiny dik-dik and other living antelopes. Physiologist John M. King of Cambridge University found that territorial stallions are the largest of the males and noted that many of them are scarred, especially on the neck, from battles with other stallions. In most instances they are older stallions. Faint enamel cups still visible on the lower central incisors indicated that one territorial stallion examined by King was about ten years old.

The Klingels' field study included ten territories established in a rainy-season grazing area near Wamba in northern Kenya. Stallions usually stake their territories in dry, rocky areas, while grazing groups of zebras occupy the flatter scrub terrain. A stallion's mere presence establishes his territory. Now and then a loud bray proclaims his land holding. Dung piles, sometimes heaped 16 inches high by repeated use, define territorial limits, as much for the stallion as for intruders. A stallion is tolerant toward other stallions and mares that cross his territorial boundaries. Within the boundaries, however, other stallions are subordinate and never challenge him.

Skirmishes between stallions occur along territorial boundaries, usually when there is an estrous mare nearby. As the two stallions fight, each tries to drive the mare toward the center of his territory. The stallion that succeeds follows the mare, while his opponent remains on his own ground. The Klingels took advantage of this aspect of Grévy's zebra behavior to determine actual boundaries of stallion territories. By using their vehicle to herd estrous mares toward boundaries they induced fights between neighboring stallions and thus were able to plot boundary lines. Stallion territories measured from 1 to 4 square miles and averaged 2.2 square miles. Grévy's zebra and wild ass stallions have the largest male territories recorded among herbivores.

In nonterritorial areas, estrous mares are pursued by numbers of stallions, sometimes as many as nine, whose continuous fighting precludes mating. Sooner or later the mare and her would-be suitors move into a solitary stallion's territory. The fact that no disputes occur when the territorial stallion mounts the mare indicates the mating function of the territories.

Stallions leave their territories only when thirst impels a trek to water. Since Grévy's zebras are less dependent upon water than plains zebras, this urge may be at intervals of several days. Often they stay behind when dry-season shortages cause mares, foals, and nonterritorial stallions to move in search of water and grass. When conditions become critical the territorial stallions migrate. But they do not establish territories in dry-season areas and therefore cannot mate with mares, a fact that restricts breeding to the rainy season. Because rains are unpredictable where Grévy's zebras live, this segregation of sexes undoubtedly influences the species' reproductive rate.

By the time the rains come, the stallions are back in their territories, well ahead of the return of the other zebras. Stallions are thought to maintain their same territories for years at a time.

MARKING BEHAVIOR

Zebras defecate and urinate on the droppings and urine of other zebras. Family stallions mark the droppings of their estrous mares. Marking also is a common occurrence among stallions in bachelor bands. Presumably this equid behavior pattern, functional only among Grévy's zebra stallions whose land holdings are staked by small manure piles, was inherited from territorial ancestors.

11. Facts of Life

ALTHOUGH stallions in zoos attain sexual maturity somewhat earlier, it is doubtful that a stallion can compete successfully for fillies and mares until he is at least five years old. In the Klingels' study the oldest colt still found with his family group was 4½ years old. The youngest stallions with mares of their own were five- to six-year-olds.

Fillies mature earlier than colts. First estrus occurs at about thirteen months. From then on, at approximately twenty-one-day intervals, a filly displays the conspicuous estrous posture, marked by slightly elevated hindquarters and raised tail. This posture combined with the ears-back, open-mouth threat expression signals her readiness for mating.

This typical estrous posture stimulates stallions, a fact learned by the Klingels when tranquilizing caused mares to assume a similar stance that immediately attracted stallions from nearby herds. While fillies maintain this estrous posture for as long as a week at a time, luring the

attentions of numbers of stallions (the Klingels counted eighteen attending one herd), mares display the posture only briefly at the height of estrus, and then only at the approach of the herd stallion. Thus this mating posture serves two functions. Persistently and conspicuously displayed by fillies, it prevents inbreeding; assumed fleetingly and inconspicuously by mares, it preserves the family group.

A filly in heat often triggers fights among stallions. Two young stallions, each trying to start his own family group, may battle. Or an older stallion may wage a bitter contest to add another filly to his group. The herd stallion meets the interloper with head outstretched and ears forward. Abruptly he threatens by raising his head, flattening his ears, and baring his teeth. The stallions circle, toss their heads, and canter about, maneuvering for position. Unless the would-be suitor is intimidated, a fight starts. Rearing, shoving, and neck-wrestling, the stallions bite at ears, neck, mane, chest, and legs, occasionally inflicting lacerations or a crushing bite. When a leg hold is obtained the zebras drop to their knees to struggle. Each tries for a hold on the other's hock as they circle on their knees. Throughout such contests the herd stallion's mares are absorbed onlookers.

Richard D. Estes, who photographed a battle between two stallions that lasted more than two hours and was waged over several miles, commented on the determination and stamina of the herd stallion's defense: "If every rival he faced was starting out completely fresh, probably it would call for more endurance than flesh and blood could provide. Fortunately for him, though, the rivals also fight with one another. But this is not enough to explain why the herd stallion almost always wins. His winning simply illustrates the principle that right makes might."

Eventually pain or exhaustion may cause one of the rivals to lie still. As soon as his opponent lets go, the stallion scrambles to his feet, ready to resume the fight. Eventually the loser gallops off, lashing out with his hindlegs if he is pursued.

Less intent skirmishes end when one stallion expresses submission by turning his head down and to one side. After a few more bites and shoves, his opponent stretches his head along the loser's croup and the fight is over.

Odors also are associated with estrus. An estrous mare urinates frequently; the stallion responds by flehming, a kind of olfactory urinalysis by which he determines the mare's reproductive status. Sniffing the urine, he inhales the scent, then raises his head, opens his mouth, and curls his upper lip in a prolonged grimace called the *Flehmen*.

Flehming forces the odor of the urine into contact with a small tubelike structure in the roof of the mouth which is lined in part with olfactory receptor cells and communicates with the nasal cavity. This vomero-nasal or Jacobson's organ is presumed to be sensitive to varying concentrations of sex hormone by-products excreted in a mare's urine. Mares sometimes perform the *Flehmen* as a greeting gesture. Even foals have been seen to flehm.

Full estrus is indicated by a mare's elevated hindquarters, tail carried to one side and the *Rossigkeitgesicht*, a term used by Trumler to describe the ears-back, open-mouth, chewing, submissive mare-in-heat facial expression. The courting stallion follows closely, sniffing, nipping, and rubbing his muzzle against the mare. Kicks in the chest and short chases after the mare do not discourage him. Sooner or later he attempts mounting. Copulation usually is repeated at one- to three-hour intervals throughout the day. During this mating time other mares show their resentment, especially if the estrous mare is a low-ranking member of the group.

Gestation among zebras takes about a year. Grévy's zebra has

the longest gestation of any equid, 390 days. Mountain zebra gestations are recorded from 300 to 365 days. A plains zebra average zoo gestation of 371 days is supported by the Klingels' finding that the shortest intervals between foaling were 378 and 385 days. In both instances the mares conceived during the so-called foal heat, the estrus that occurs a few days after foaling. More often there is a foaling-conception interval of one month.

12. Mares and Foals

FOALING occurs throughout the year. However, rainy-season peaks that coincide with good grazing conditions are apparent. In Ngorongoro the main foaling season is January to March, when more than 80 percent of the foals are born. In the Serengeti, foaling peaks during January and February, but only 61 percent of the foals are dropped then. February is foaling time for most mares in Kenya's Nairobi National Park. The Klingels found foaling also correlated with rainfall distribution among zebra herds they studied in Etosha, Kruger, and Wankie national parks in southern Africa.

Grévy's zebra mares usually foal in August or September. Perhaps because they are larger than their plains zebra relatives, their in-foal condition is more obvious.

Distension of belly, swollen vulva, raised tail, and restricted hind-leg gait indicate parturition time. The mare moves off from the herd. Birth is a dangerous time for prey species. But a plains zebra mare is watched over by the herd stallion who stands 10 or more yards away, ready to drive off any predators or scavengers. Some 50 yards away the rest of the family group grazes.

Soon two tiny hoofs project from the mare's birth canal, followed by a small nose tightly pressed against long forelegs. Usually in this second stage of labor the mare lies down. Expulsion of the fetus, partly enveloped in its amniotic sac and with umbilical cord still intact, takes seven or eight minutes. Sometimes a mare does it differently and parturition takes longer. Kenyan naturalist Anthony Cullen recorded an observation of two Tanzanian game rangers in *Window onto Wilderness*: "At the start of the birth, the zebra lay down, but when half way through the process the mother stood up and the foal was dropped. Birth took place in about fifteen minutes."

The newborn foal shakes its head, then wriggles to free its front end from the amniotic membrane, ruptured in the birth process. With fore-

66

legs extended it pushes its way to its mother's head. The mare licks her foal's nostrils, eyes, and ears, ingesting birth fluids that may be important in establishing the mare-foal bond. Ethologist Jane Goodall suggested the possible bonding function of this maternal act after an unfortunate incident in the Serengeti when she happened on a mare that had just foaled. The mare scrambled to her feet and left her foal struggling on the ground. Goodall backed her vehicle some 100 yards away and remained to watch. The foal managed to free itself from the birth sac and got up. But the mare joined a group of zebras, presumably her family group, 60 yards off and did not return to the foal. Instead she wandered away with the group. Four hours later the foal was still alone, trying to suckle on a fallen tree. "We saw many zebras pass by, but the foal left its 'tree mother' for none of them."

Usually the mare gets on her feet, sniffs at her foal, and licks its hindquarters. The foal tries again and again to stand up. Eleven minutes after birth the foal is on its feet. At nineteen minutes it totters. By thirty-two minutes it walks well; by forty-four minutes it canters. An hour after being born the foal frisks and runs. This seems a short time to get such a small, thin body on long legs in motion. Yet hoofed mammals that are not born into the protection of a tight-knit family group accomplish the process in even less time. Within five minutes of its birth a wildebeest calf is up and running.

The foal's legs are long, especially long below knee and hock; its trunk and neck are short; its croup is higher than its withers; its forehead is rounded; and its hoofs are tiny. A wispy mane runs along neck and back to the base of its short, brushy tail. Long, soft body hairs give its dark brown and white striped coat a fuzzy appearance. It weighs about 60 or 70 pounds.

A Grévy's zebra foal, usually born into a nursery group of mares with foals, weighs in at about 90 pounds and stands nearly 3 feet at the withers. Large-eared and spindly-legged, the thin-bodied foal is covered with woolly hair. Its light-brown stripes are darker on head, neck, and legs. Its mane continues behind the withers, along the back, and over the croup to the tail. This spinal mane disappears after a few weeks, except for a persistent area on the croup. At eight months the foal's stripes are dark gray-brown and it stands about 13.2 hands high. A month later it is weaned.

When just over an hour old, the foal suckles from one of the two teats on its mother's swollen milk bag. At this stage a foal will follow any moving object. For this reason the mare, with lowered head and flattened ears, fends off the approach of other zebras. After a few days the mare-foal bond is firmly established. The foal stays close to its dam, apparently able to recognize her by scent, stripe pattern, and call, and the mare's threatening behavior ceases.

It was before this critical bonding had formed between mare and foal that Daphne Sheldrick, wife of the game warden in charge of Kenya's vast Tsavo East National Park, acquired one of her famous orphans. The Sheldricks were driving in the park one evening when suddenly they noticed a zebra foal struggling to keep up with their Land Rover. They stopped and the foal trotted up within a few paces. It stood by while the Sheldricks searched the dry-bush landscape for its mother. While David Sheldrick stayed with the foal, his wife drove back to camp for help. She returned with the rangers to find the foal trotting along the track at the warden's heels. When he stopped the foal pressed against him for security. Thus the bond was established between the Sheldricks and the orphan Huppety.

Foals frisk and play, sometimes with colts and fillies from other nearby family groups. Play is important, for it imitates the serious activities of zebra life, involves body control, and perfects responses to young zebras' physical and social environment. Sometimes an adult zebra chases a foal in play. Occasionally foals pursue other animals. The Klingels saw a foal chase a frightened mongoose into its hole.

Plains zebra foals are weaned at about seven months. Some four months after her foal is weaned, a zebra mare may give birth again. Mares are capable of producing a foal every year; however, rainfall, burning patterns, disease, malnutrition, population density, and predator pressure influence birth as well as survival rates among zebras. The Klingels tallied only 48.1 percent of the Ngorongoro mares and 34.1 percent of the Serengeti mares with foals of the previous season.

GRÉVY'S FOAL

PLAINS FOAL

PLAINS FOAL

PLAINS FOAL

13. Daily Activities

JUST after sunrise zebras and their wildebeest companions move to their grazing grounds, trekking single file along narrow game paths that crisscross the plains. In fact, moving to grazing areas and grazing take up much of zebras' time. Continuous feeders (as opposed to occasional feeders like lions), they fill their digestive tracts daily with large quantities of food that has comparatively little nutritive value. Grazing interludes are taken up with such activities as mutual grooming, visits to rubbing or rolling places, treks to water, and in bachelor bands, skirmishing. Usually there is an early afternoon rest period when zebras often rest their heads on each other's backs, a gesture of friendliness as well as a safety position that gives each zebra twosome a 360-degree view of the surroundings. As dusk approaches, zebras and wildebeests move out into open, short-grass areas where they will spend the night.

GRAZING

On the African plains conflict among herbivores is avoided and overgrazing prevented by the fact that each browser or grazer uses a different type of vegetation, or uses the same vegetation but at a different time of year, or uses a different level of the same vegetation, or prefers a different habitat (riverine thickets or open areas of short grass). In other words, no two plains herbivore species overlap in total feeding requirements.

Zebras are the only plains grazers that have upper as well as lower incisors that enable them to bite off rather than pluck grasses. This is probably why they crop taller, coarser grass. A study of stomach contents and droppings by Serengeti Research Institute ecologist Richard H. V. Bell showed that although zebras and wildebeests move together and feed on the same kinds of grasses, they do not graze the same stage of growth. Tall grass is more stem (hard, fibrous, and cellulose-containing) than lower leafy grass (soft and high in protein content).

With a digestive system well adapted for large intake of roughage, zebras prefer grass at this stage; the antelopes find it too tough.

Zebras, topis, wildebeests, and Thomson's gazelles often feed on the same grasses. Zebras graze down the coarse taller grasses, trampling much of what they do not eat. Topis, with their pointed muzzles, reach for lower parts of stems. Wildebeests use their square muzzles to pluck shorter grasses and horizontal grass leaves. The shortest, most succulent plants and newly sprouted grasses are delicately nibbled by the small gazelles. When the grass has been cropped short most of the grazers move on and do not return until rains bring fresh growth.

The most common association of African herbivores is that of plains zebras and wildebeests (or brindled gnus). In fact, wildebeests are not often seen without zebras. The large-headed gray wildebeests occur

in southern Kenya and parts of Tanzania. They are bearded, black or white depending upon subspecies, and have long-haired black tails. Dark bands on neck and forequarters give them a brindled appearance. Loud moaning grunts, punctuated by occasional explosive snorts, sound from their herds, always on the move in search of the right grazing conditions. Often with wildebeests and zebras are the little rufous-fawn, tail-flicking tommies (Thomson's gazelles).

Other zebra grazing companions include kongonis or Coke's hartebeests, impalas, Grant's gazelles, giraffes, elephants, buffaloes, and warthogs. There is some safety to be gained when ungulate groups mingle. Not only is each species sensitive to the alarm response of at least some of the others, but in large mixed assemblages there are more eyes to watch, ears to swivel, and nostrils to test for sight, sound, and scent of approaching predators. Zebras must sense this security, for in large herds they appear to be less alert.

Zebras also associate with oryxes. In Kenya's Tsavo and Amboseli national parks plains zebras sometimes are seen with fringe-eared

oryxes. Grévy's zebras often mingle with the paler gray beisa oryxes, a northern subspecies that shares their range. Waterbucks, elands, and kudus are other Grévy's zebra grazing companions.

In South Africa white-tailed gnus (or black wildebeests), quaggas, and ostriches once were a common sight. This gnu, with a curious upward-pointing, brushlike tuft of stiff hairs on its muzzle, a bearded throat and tuft of hairs between its forelegs, and flowing white tail, was known as "the old fool of the veld" because of its clownlike antics. Bellowing snorts, shying, plunging, and wild flurries of bucks and kicks always accompanied its dashes across the plains.

Ostriches frequently associate with zebra herds, perhaps benefiting them as long-necked sentries. Cattle egrets or buff-backed herons stalk beside the forelegs of grazing zebras to snap up insects disturbed from the grass. Oxpeckers pick ticks from zebra hides and often maintain open sores. At water holes zebras sometimes join woolly storks, crowned cranes, or a 4-foot-tall saddle-bill stork stalking in the shallows.

MUTUAL GROOMING

Social grooming, which once had a cooperative cleaning function, has become ritualized and serves as a group bonding device. Two zebras approach. Their upper lips are extended. Standing shoulder to shoulder, they begin nibbling with their incisor teeth on each other's neck and back, places a zebra cannot reach on its own body. As if on signal both zebras step back, their heads swing, and they step forward again to groom the other side. Grooming sessions last from a few minutes to half an hour.

Mares groom with their foals. Stallions show preference in grooming some mares more than others. The stallion alone grooms with a new mare or filly in his group. In all instances mutual grooming cements bonds between group members.

The Klingels kept six zebras in the course of their study, at first taming them by grooming the orphaned foals and older animals with a brush attached to a long stick. The zebras readily submitted to this currying and brushing and in no time the brush could be handheld. Estes has speculated that this response, "based on social grooming, a fundamental equine trait, may well have a bearing on the original domestication of the horse and ass, and the unusual tolerance of these animals toward being handled."

Although vigorous rubbing accompanies their greeting ceremonies, mountain zebras are reported not to indulge in social grooming. Rarely do Grévy's zebras groom each other; however, a stallion in the Frankfurt zoo staged mutual grooming sessions with his keeper and with some less-indulgent Watusi cattle that shared his enclosure.

SHUDDERING AND SHAKING

Zebras fight to rid themselves of flies by shuddering, or twitching their skin. This is accomplished by contraction of part of a thin muscular layer, the cutaneous muscle, that is closely attached to the skin of shoulders, forearms, back, and flanks. This muscle is not developed on hindquarters where annoying insects are within reach of a swishing tail.

Shaking is another method of getting rid of insects, water (after rain), and dust (after rolling).

ROLLING AND RUBBING

Like all equids, zebras take delight in rolling and rubbing to remove loose hairs and dead skin from their bodies. Because of their well-rounded shapes zebras are good rollers, able to roll completely over and back again, a pleasure denied their humpbacked wildebeest com-

panions. This seems particularly unfair since wildebeests stamp bare the
areas of ground that are the zebras' favorite dust wallows. Probably because of its higher croup, a mountain zebra first rolls on one side, gets
up, goes down again, and then rolls on the other side.

Large rocks and tree trunks, upright or fallen, are used for rubbing.
These rubbing objects are few and far between on the plains and often
zebras queue up for a chance to rub their necks, sides, bellies, and
rumps.

Termite mounds, or anthills as they are called, are a blessing to
hoofed animals. These many-chambered, thin-walled structures are

strong enough to withstand use as sentry posts by hartebeests. Rhinoceroses scrape and shape their horns on termite mounds. Zebras use them for rubbing. They straddle small mounds to rub bellies and between-legs, and back under tall leaning mounds to rub ticks from around the bases of their tails or to relieve the itching caused by internal parasites.

Zebras also rub their heads against their forelegs, use hind hoofs to scratch their heads, and even rub one hindleg against the other. Foals rub against their mothers' bellies and legs.

WATER

With first light of day gazelles come to water. Somewhat later, usually between eight and eleven, come zebras and wildebeests. Water holes, often formed where tree-shrouded rivers widen, provide opportunity for lions that have not killed at night. Aware of the danger of ambush, zebras approach with caution and suspicion. They move forward, stop, proceed 100 yards more, halt. A few zebras advance, stand motionless, then wheel about and trot back to the others. Again the herd moves forward. Nervously the zebras make their way along well-trodden paths through thick underbrush. Once more they halt. Then, apparently satisfied there is no cause for alarm, they head down the riverbank.

Muzzles are plunged deep into the water and ears flick as the zebras drink through closed teeth. Those standing in the shallows are pushed by zebras behind. Reluctant to move into deeper water where a crocodile's jaws can mean sudden death, they protest with squeals and kicks. Now and again heads raise and muzzles drip as zebras keep watch.

At water holes an adaptive shift occurs in family groups. The stallion that has led his mares and foals to water allows the dominant mare to leave first. He brings up the rear, placing himself between his family and the danger of attack by a lurking predator.

Where zebras drink at water holes that are spring-fed or man-made (as in many of the parks), their single-file approach shows little hesitation.

SKIRMISHES

During the last few hours of daylight zebras and other plains herbivores are most active. As the herds return from grazing grounds to their short-grass sleeping areas, play skirmishes and vigorous fights often break out

among colts and stallions. Scuffles also occur at water holes or when a bachelor band comes too close to a family group.

In zoo situations fighting is not restricted to stallion contests. When the Frankfurt zoo added two Grévy's zebra mares to its collection, the stallion that shared his paddock with the Watusi cattle began to skirmish with the bulls. In zebra fashion he bit at their napes and legs, jumped on them, and kicked them. Retaliating with heads lowered in bovid fashion, the bulls tried to impale him. After each bout, the stallion chased after the cows and their calves. Eventually it was decided to move the three zebras to another enclosure.

SLEEPING

Zebras rest and sleep during the night. Young animals lie down for complete rest; older zebras lie down less often and for shorter times. To lie down, the zebra gathers its four legs under its body, flexes its knees and hocks, and flops down on one side, its legs folded on the opposite side and its upright head and neck curved over its forelegs. For a short time it may stretch out on its side. To get up, the zebra extends its forelegs and rises first in front. With a powerful thrust of its hindlegs it is on its feet. Usually a vigorous shake and sometimes a stretch follow getting up. A foal that has napped in its mother's shadow stretches its neck and first one hindleg, then the other.

While zebras rest there is always at least one herd member alert and on its feet. Often the family stallion stands watch while his mares

and foals lie down, close together. On a moonlit night, while trailing hyenas in Ngorongoro, Jane Goodall saw a zebra group and was "impressed by the obvious alertness of the sentinel and the apparently relaxed slumber of the others." Between their several nighttime rest periods zebras graze.

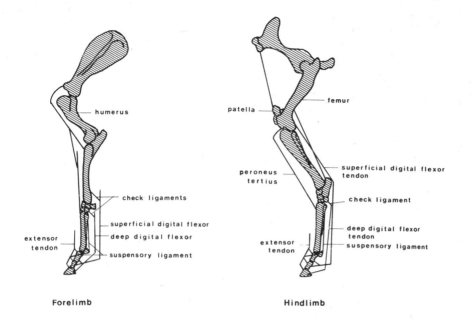

Forelimb · Hindlimb

TENDONS AND LIGAMENTS

Tendons and ligaments making up the stay apparatus that enables a zebra to stand while it sleeps. (After Sisson and Grossman. *The Anatomy of the Domestic Animals.* Philadelphia: W. B. Saunders Co., 1953.)

Occasionally a zebra lies down during the day. Its sleep may be so sound that it is left behind. Suddenly it scrambles to its feet, looks about, and gallops after its family group.

Zebras also sleep on their feet. The equid limb, standing at rest, is in a state of equilibrium. A system of opposing tendons and ligaments which counterbalance each other makes up a unique stay apparatus in each limb, enabling an equid to stand while it sleeps. The stifle or patella, acting as a lock mechanism, slides upward to engage an articular surface on the femur. Lower down, reciprocal action of the peroneus tertius (a tendinous muscle which mechanically flexes the hock when the stifle is flexed) and the superficial digital flexor (which extends the hock joint) causes the hock also to lock. Check ligaments, fibrous white bands, two in each foreleg and one in each hindleg, further reduce muscle strain when a zebra dozes on its feet. Often a hindleg is rested by flexion of its joints so that only the toe of the hoof rests on the ground.

14. Dispersal and Migration

ZEBRAS IN NGORONGORO

Ngorongoro is a huge saucerlike caldera, formed by a collapsed volcano. Within its 100 square miles of grassland, marshes, and lake, surrounded by a steep, 2,000-foot crater wall, live an estimated 25,000 herbivores, a figure that includes 5,000 to 6,000 plains zebras (the subspecies known as Böhm's zebra). The zebras form large herds that move about according to seasonal changes in habitat and grazing conditions.

Each of the herds uses a common sleeping ground, always in an open dry area of short grass, for resting at night. In late afternoon thousands of zebras and wildebeests congregate on the central plains. Except in the rainy season when they appear reluctant to leave their sleeping grounds, mornings find the zebras moving off to grazing areas.

By June, after the long rains, the sleeping grounds are near the large soda lake and the zebras feed on long grass that flourishes on the crater floor. In August, later in the dry season, the herds' sleeping grounds are near the southern wall of the crater. Then the zebras make daily treks of up to 8 miles to graze on the slopes and along drying-up edges of swamps on the crater floor. By October, near the end of the dry season, the zebra population is split into seven herds, each with its own sleeping ground, and grazing is restricted to the still green vegetation of dried-up swamps.

DRY-SEASON FIRES

Part of the African plains scene, fires, sometimes ignited by lightning and more often by the Masai and other pastoralists, help to maintain grassland free of scrubby vegetation. As the dry season progresses hundreds of fires burn. Flames consume the dry grass, but the deep roots are not harmed. Grazing conditions are altered as new growth sprouts. Zebras are among the first grazers to return to a burned area.

86

RAINS

Toward the end of the long dry season when the wind smells of dust and the dry grass crackles there is a sudden discernible increase in humidity. Ever-changing clouds tower up, fill the sky, and travel with the wind. Even before any rain falls acacia trees blossom and leaf. Zebras sense the excitement of the coming rain. Possibly they are sensitive to barometric pressure or to wind and temperature changes. Zebra herds have been known to gallop with wildebeests toward a rainstorm nearly 5 miles away. By night zebras sometimes travel 25 miles to reach a feeding area where rains have caused new grass to sprout and surface water to fill water holes.

Over much of East Africa rain falls in two seasons. Distance from the equator, and from the sea, and altitude modify these rainy seasons, one of which is longer and wetter (the long rains) than the other (the short rains). Climatic changes during the year cause changes in food and water supplies that in turn affect many of the animals.

In northern Kenya, where rains are not always predictable, seasonal movements cause shifts in actual zebra numbers as well as changes in relative numbers of plains zebras and Grévy's zebras. The short rains signal southward migration from the Leroghi Plateau and the Wamba area to south of the Uaso Nyiro River where the zebras remain on floodplain grasslands until they trek north again during the long dry months.

In Ngorongoro the short rains that usually come in November and December cause some new grass to sprout. They also cause dispersal. In November some 1,500 of the zebras travel up out of the crater along ancient game trails that traverse its walls. When the zebras return the following May, at the beginning of the dry season, the zebra population once again forms three nonstable herds.

ZEBRAS IN THE SERENGETI

Some 150,000 plains zebras roam the Serengeti, a vast region of plains and hills, open woodlands as well as grassland, that lies between the Crater Highlands and Lake Victoria in northern Tanzania. Rains are more or less predictable in the Serengeti and cause regular large-scale migrations, seasonal spectacles in which zebras take part. George Schaller described zebras on the move: "They stream by, their black and white columns in the flat light making one so dizzy from the motion that only the zebra appear stable in the moving world."

With the coming of the rains, Böhm's zebras migrate from the Mara woodlands of southern Kenya, where there is water all year, back to the Serengeti plains. Their herds move ahead of and straggle behind the long armylike columns of wildebeests. Some zebras stay behind, in groups scattered throughout the Mara woodlands during the rainy season.

HOME RANGE

Every zebra group has a home range, a large area over which it roams in the course of its normal activities. Zebra home ranges overlap. But within each home range, of family group or bachelor band, the zebras move freely and independently of other zebras.

From observations of marked animals and their groups the Klingels plotted home ranges of Ngorongoro zebras that varied in extent from 30 to nearly 100 square miles.

A zebra group that roams the Serengeti during the long rainy season (March to May) finds an abundance of good grazing and has a large home range, estimated by the Klingels to be about 100 to 150 square miles. The home range of this same zebra group increases in extent when the herds migrate 50 to 100 miles north to spend the dry season (June to October) in the Mara woodlands, where it wanders over an area of 150 to 250 square miles. Considering both grazing and migration patterns, the Klingels determined the total home range of a Serengeti zebra group to be more than 400 square miles.

15. Where Species Ranges Overlap

GRÉVY'S zebra is a characteristic member of the Somali Arid fauna of northeastern Kenya. Its counterpart in the East Africa grassland fauna is the plains zebra. The ranges of these two species meet and overlap in an area to the north of the Kenya Highlands and along the Tana River where, noted Roosevelt and Heller in 1922, Grévy's zebras "mix freely with the oryx herds and the smaller species of zebra—but they never breed with the latter."

In 1965 Allen Keast, a biologist at Queen's University in Ontario, published his observations of Grévy's zebras and plains zebras in this zone of overlap. Near Isiolo in Kenya Grévy's zebras find typical habitat on the arid plateau and rocky slopes north of the Uaso Nyiro River. Plains zebras (Grant's subspecies) roam the undulating grasslands of the Kenya Highlands south of the river. On broad, grassy river flats and shrubby grassland floodplains both species are numerous and frequently form mixed herds.

Grévy's zebras stand out like horses among ponies in these mixed herds. Keast estimated that about two-thirds of the zebras he counted in the Isiolo-Uaso Nyiro region during July were in mixed herds. Of this number, nearly three-quarters were Grévy's zebras. Only in a few smaller herds did plains zebras outnumber their larger companions.

Two large herds consisted of 250 and 160 zebras. Within the herd of 160 (125 Grévy's zebras and 36 plains zebras) the smaller species often formed two or three groups, a tendency that was most noticeable when the herd filed to or from water. Presumably these were family groups and bachelor bands. Although alarm caused the zebras in this herd to gallop off as a unit, the "numerically inferior" species kept to the center of the fleeing herd. On one occasion a single Grévy's zebra stallion sought safety in the midst of a small group of plains zebras.

Mixed herds graze during the morning, rest in shade during mid-day, and in midafternoon trek to water, and then graze again. Skirmishes and sexual activity often occur when the zebras are bunched together at the river. Always the outbreaks involve two zebras of the same species. Possibly the stripe patterns of the two species, and especially the conspicuous difference in their rump-stripe patterns, are a means of species recognition, precluding aggressive or sexual behavior between the two kinds of zebra.

This mutual tolerance between species in mixed herds is comparable to the association of plains zebras and wildebeests. But unlike such grazing assemblages, the mixed herds of zebras are marked by cohesion and constancy. Several of the small herds contained the same number of zebras throughout the month of Keast's observations. Even the large herd of 160 remained constant in its combination of the two species.

An entirely different zebra association exists in the Kaokoveld of South West Africa and in southwestern Angola where the ranges of Hartmann's mountain zebra and plains zebra (the subspecies known as the Damaraland zebra) overlap. Although the two species graze in proximity, their herds keep strictly to themselves. This apparent segregation may be due to the mountain zebra's adaptation to its mountain habitat and its tendency to range in small groups.

16. Parasites, Diseases, and Injury

VARIOUS external parasites annoy zebras. Ticks attach to their hides and gorge on their blood. Grubs or fly larvae sometimes thrive in small sacs beneath their skin. Flies are always bothersome. A few kinds cause trouble by laying their eggs in open sores. Others just suck blood.

No amount of vigorous stamping and skin twitching deters botflies from depositing their eggs on zebra forelegs. Scratching and licking by the zebra stimulates hatching. The larvae migrate into the mouth and work their way down into the zebra's stomach where they burrow into the lining. Subsequently they migrate through surrounding tissues. When maturity is reached, after some eleven months inside the zebra, the larvae pass out with the feces, flies develop, lay more eggs, and the cycle is continuous.

As new arrivals in zoos zebras sometimes are heavily infested with nematodes or roundworms of several kinds. Among them is *Strongylus vulgaris*, the most devastating of all equine parasites. As bloodsucking adults these bloodworms or redworms attach to walls of a zebra's large intestine. Female strongyles deposit enormous quantities of eggs which are eliminated with the droppings. The larvae hatch, attach to blades of grass, and are swallowed by a grazing zebra. Migrating within the zebra's body the larvae often cause local irritation and damage arteries that supply the intestinal tract. Occasionally they reduce the blood flow so that colic results. Marked by gas pains or cramping, this equid equivalent of stomachache is always serious because of the animals' inability to vomit. Massive strongyle infestations may also cause a chronic type of enteritis or inflammation of the intestines and outward signs of poor condition.

Parascaris is another roundworm parasite whose embryo-containing eggs are ingested by grazing zebras. Once the eggs reach the small intestine they hatch. The larvae burrow into the wall, penetrate capillaries, and travel in the bloodstream to the lungs. The larvae grow and molt, leave the lungs, and migrate up the trachea or windpipe where they are swallowed and returned to the small intestine to develop through maturity.

Dictyocaulus, a lung worm, sometimes infests zebras. Also nematode parasites are the pinworms found in equid large intestines. The eggs, picked up in grazing, hatch. As the larvae mature in the large intestine and the worms pass out through the rectum they irritate the dock or under-tail area, causing the zebra to rub its tail.

The muscles of zebras and other herbivores often are encysted with the larvae of various tapeworms. The cycle of these flatworms is completed when a predator consumes the flesh, allowing the larvae to develop into worms in its intestines. Tapeworm eggs are then eliminated in the predator's feces to begin the cycle again when ingested by another grazing herbivore host.

Anthrax, a severe infectious bacterial disease, affects zebras as well as other herbivores. A zebra that has anthrax appears dejected and suffers chills, colicky pains, and skin lesions. Dragging leg motion indicates the muscle weakness that accompanies this usually fatal disease.

Like other wild animals of Africa, zebras are immune to trypanosomiasis, a disease caused by one-celled trypanosomes, blood parasites that become infective in the mouth parts of tsetse flies and are transmitted when a fly bites an animal. Trypanosomes cause various kinds of sleeping sickness in man and his domestic animals. The parasites do not normally affect a wild animal in good condition. Even as carriers of this disease zebras have some immunity, for tsetse flies prefer the dark hides of buffaloes, elephants, warthogs, and rhinoceroses to zebras' striped ones. Nevertheless, thousands of zebras have been slaughtered in wide-scale attempts to control the wild animal carriers of trypanosomiasis.

Like horses, zebras may be susceptible to tetanus. This disease is caused by a bacillus, or large rodlike bacterium, in soil or manure. Growing only in the absence of oxygen, it produces a powerful nerve poison once it gains entry into a deep puncture or claw wound. Convulsive muscle contractions result and in horses death almost invariably

follows. But resistance may enable zebras, as it does their donkey relatives, to survive a bout with tetanus.

Torn flaps of skin and long scratches or bite marks on a zebra come
from maulings by predators. Zebras also inflict injury on their own
kind. Much biting and kicking goes on at water holes. When a powerful
kick connects, a broken leg or jaw may be the result, a serious mishap for
any equid. Occasionally an aardvark hole or warthog den may cause a
galloping zebra to fall and break a leg.

Zebras have been reported to survive broken limbs in spite of ever
watchful predators and probably because of the security of the herd. As
they move about from place to place the other zebras in the group wait
for the injured animal to catch up. With time the broken limb sets and
heals, though often at an odd angle.

Zebras in captivity have also survived broken legs. A six-year-old
Grévy's zebra stallion in the National Zoological Park sustained a double fracture of a rear cannon bone. Zoo veterinarian Clinton W. Gray
immobilized, anesthetized, x-rayed, and reduced the fracture, and ap-
plied a walking cast. After twelve weeks the cast was removed and the
stallion regained normal use of his hindleg.

17. Predators, Scavengers, and Man

IN the course of evolution zebras have been shaped by predators. Adaptations of form and behavior, developed through time and in response to constant predator pressure, include their bulging eyes, their long flicking ears, their large flaring nostrils, their swift running ability, and their tendency to form herds. Predator-prey relations are so closely bound that without one the other could not exist. Predators benefit prey animals by keeping their numbers within the carrying capacity of their habitat. They also weed out unfit animals from the herds. Without predators to keep their populations in check, prey species suffer the drastic tolls of disease and starvation.

Zebra lives, like those of any prey species, always hang in balance. There is a tension about zebras in the wild, marked by bright eyes, poise of head on curve of neck, alert stance, even the flick of an ear. Yet zebras are not always alert. Of necessity their behavior wavers between avoiding predators and attaining their daily needs. When stalked, ambushed, or chased by predators, their responses come from long inbred reaction patterns rather than fear.

Herd formation is the zebra's most obvious antipredator device. Small herds offer greater safety than large ones. Not only are zebras in large herds apt to be careless but, as Schaller observed in the course of his three-year study of lions in the Serengeti, "when many zebra are packed in a tight mass around a water-hole, they get in one another's way when attacked, giving a lion that extra fraction of a second advantage that may mean the difference between success and failure in a hunt." Even the habit of moving from place to place in single file, common among all members of the horse family, is a behavioral defense mechanism that lessens the chance of a zebra's coming upon a crouched predator.

A zebra foal is born into the security of a small, closely protected family unit. When predators appear, the mare with a young foal moves behind the other family members; her foal presses close to her side. In this way the foal learns what evasive action to take when a predator is detected. It also learns to distinguish the walking and stalking positions of lions, and to be wary of hyenas, wild dogs, and even the cheetah, predators that specialize in killing young animals.

While mares and foals bunch together, the stallion aggressively attacks the hyenas or wild dogs that threaten his family. Even lions on occasion have been beaten off or severely injured by zebra stallions. The South African artist-naturalist Charles T. Astley Maberly recorded the finding of a man's mutilated body: "From the tracks it appeared that he had killed a zebra foal, and the whole troop had attacked him and bitten and kicked him to death."

LIONS

Except in Ngorongoro, where they are outnumbered by hyenas, lions are the chief predators of zebras. Zebras are second only to wildebeests in lion-kill percentages. Long-bodied, short-necked, and heavy-limbed, lions have well-padded feet with retractable claws and short jaws with stabbing canine teeth. Like all cats, they capture prey through stealth, by stalk or ambush. Sight, hearing, and smell, in that order, are the senses used by hunting lions.

When a lion hunts during the day it lies in ambush, usually near a water hole. Sometimes a lioness lies hidden in a thicket for half a day, waiting for a zebra herd on the plains to come to water. Sooner or later the zebras come. If the lioness has guessed their route to the water hole and if her tawny body is well concealed, she will have a chance to lunge as the last zebras pass by.

Like most predators, lions are opportunists, always alert for young, sick, injured, aged, or in any way odd-appearing or careless prey animals. Schaller watched as a male lion, ambling across the plains, spotted a zebra foal "so deeply asleep on the grass that it even failed to hear the alarm snorts of its family. The lion wakened it briefly." And he witnessed another instance of unexpected hunting when a sick and solitary zebra made its slow way past a resting pride and was killed. Old zebras (in the wild "old" is about twelve years) often are victims of lions. Schaller admitted surprise when, nearing the completion of his field work, he lined up the zebra skulls he had collected at lion kills. A check of the teeth showed a large proportion of the skulls were those of old zebras, possibly animals that were less agile and fleet. But lions also hunt alert, healthy zebras.

In late afternoon lions stir and stretch. Cubs in the pride are playful. As Schaller has noted, "Pride males are rather reticent about expending their energy in hunting." So the pride's females do most (80 percent or more) of the hunting, supplying meat for themselves, their cubs, and the males that are only temporary members of a pride. The fact is that, being larger and more powerful and conspicuously maned,

lions may be needed to stay behind and protect the pride's cubs from marauding hyenas. Males that are nomadic or not attached to a pride make their own kills.

Two lionesses sit up. They stare intently at a distant herd of prey animals. One of them moves off to crouch concealed in low bushes. She continues her stalk only when the zebras she watches are grazing or have their heads turned away from her. Tension marks her stalk, and patience, for much of the time her stalk is interrupted by long periods of crouching and waiting. Where cover is sufficient a lion may get close enough (within 30 yards) to rush from concealment and in a flurry of violence bring down a zebra. But this lioness waits, keeping the zebras under observation, until darkness falls.

Cooperation increases hunting success. So does stalking upwind instead of downwind, although with lions this is a matter of chance. In group hunting lionesses fan out in an irregular line toward their selected prey. Sometimes their cooperation appears deliberate; in other instances it may be accidental.

Surprise is an important factor when lions hunt. Fearful of sharp hoofs and hurtling bodies, lions never attack head on, but always from the rear or side. During her stalk and before her rush the lioness must adjust her line of approach to the zebra's speed. When she has judged accurately she hooks a forepaw into the fleeing zebra's rump or flank, jerking the animal off its feet. Unless the zebra is at once overwhelmed, the lioness risks injury from flailing hoofs. She grabs for the zebra's throat to hold on for as long as eight to thirteen minutes until the strangling zebra ceases to move. Less often a lion suffocates its victim by closing its mouth over the animal's muzzle. Terming lions tidy if not quick killers, Schaller estimated their plains zebra hunting success rate to be 27 percent.

On occasion a zebra's well-aimed kick has broken a lion's jaw. Once caught, however, a zebra makes no attempt to defend itself. Even when standing with spread forelegs, squealing and resisting the clumsy efforts of a lion to topple it, a zebra makes no effort to kick or bite.

The carcass may be eaten at the kill site or dragged off a short way. The pride assembles at the kill. Sooner or later the large-maned males of the pride appear. Their presence sometimes is necessary to discourage or dispel hyenas that attempt to drive lions from their kills. However, in Ngorongoro, where the hyena population is dense, lions feed almost entirely on hyena kills.

There is much snarling and cuffing as lions lie flank to flank, feeding. Usually intestines are consumed first, with a sucking technique that expresses their contents. Then, using their carnassial shears (formed on either side of their jaws by upper fourth premolar and lower first molar), the lions cut through skin and connective tissue. Long canines tear out chunks of muscle; incisors nibble at and pull free smaller pieces of meat. According to Schaller, "lions bolt meat so rapidly that if many are present only the skeleton of a zebra may be left after 30 minutes."

SPOTTED HYENAS

Hyenas are scraggly animals with large heads, massive jaws that contain bone-crunching teeth, powerful forequarters, sloping backs, and weak hindquarters. Their curious tails, often carried between their legs, are flipped up when they are alert and aggressive. Although their gait is an ungainly lope, hyenas can run up to 40 miles an hour and maintain a slower steady lope for miles.

Like most carnivores, hyenas scavenge (eat carrion or snatch prey from other predators). This is the hyena's habit by day. When not sleeping in a comfortable mudhole or warthog den, or under a bush, a hyena scans the sky for spiraling vultures that signal a carcass, or trails a hunting pack of wild dogs for the chance to snatch their quarry.

Well equipped for their role as plains undertakers, hyenas have three blunt, bone-splintering premolars on either side of their upper and lower jaws and strong digestive juices that completely reduce bone fragments in their stomach. In no time skeletal remains are converted into white, powdery, calcium-laden droppings.

Hans Kruuk of Oxford University made a seven-year study of hyenas in the Serengeti and in Ngorongoro Crater that revealed much about their clan organization and hunting behavior. The large, female-dominated clans are highly territorial in Ngorongoro and less territorial in the Serengeti where hyenas often must follow migrating herds.

Clans gather in late afternoon. Endless greetings are exchanged among the hyenas. After dark their loud *ooooo-whup* rallying calls and chuckles sound. Night transforms hyenas from scavengers to predators.

Zebras, wildebeests, and gazelles are preferred prey of hyenas. Each is hunted with a different technique. A single hyena hunts gazelles. One or two hyenas set off to hunt wildebeests. But when zebras are to be chased a pack of up to twenty-five (average size, eleven) forms. Kruuk is convinced that hyenas have adopted pack hunting in response to aggressive defense by zebra family stallions.

A hyena pack of fourteen makes its way through a large wildebeest herd and walks slowly toward a zebra family group that has reacted by forming a semicircle. Heads up and ears forward, the zebras stare as the hyenas approach to within 10 yards. While hunting lions are kept at distances of over 150 feet, zebras exhibit a low fleeing distance for hyenas (and wild dogs). This difference may be due to the stalk or ambush hunting technique of lions and the coursing methods of capture used by the other two predators.

The hyenas continue their slow advance. Mares and foals bunch up and turn to walk away. The stallion, head lowered and ears flattened, charges. The hyenas, no match for his biting teeth and flashing hoofs, scatter amid giggles and yells. Then, as the stallion viciously strikes at individual hyenas, there is chaos. Barking excitedly, the zebra family gallops off.

Trailing his family, the stallion turns repeatedly to charge the hyenas that pursue now in crescent formation. Five hyenas run behind him, three move to cut him off from his mares. The stallion slows. Sensing he has fallen behind, the group wheels and stops. Renewing his attack on the hyenas, the stallion chases them around the tightly bunched mares and foals. The hyenas dodge his lunges and turn their attention to the other zebras.

Again the zebras move off at a canter. More hyenas join the chase. Each hyena hunts for itself, attempting to bite any zebra it can reach. A mare is grabbed, but the hyena loses its grip. Suddenly a yearling is grabbed, slowed and pulled down. Other hyenas converge and because of their numbers the young zebra's death by disemboweling is quick.

At their kill, hyenas are rapid eaters. Kruuk saw a zebra mare and yearling foal, killed after a chase by twenty-five hyenas, disappear entirely in less than forty minutes. Hyenas are noisy on a kill, but there is little fighting. They gulp down enormous quantities of meat, as much as 30 pounds or a third of their body weight. Often a leg or head is torn off and carried away to be eaten, or stored in shallow water.

Possibly one-third of hyena pack hunts end in the killing of a zebra. Often hyenas chase zebras in vain. Jane Goodall followed a Ngorongoro hunt by Land Rover when some 200 zebras, family groups and bachelor bands that had congregated for the night, were pursued by a pack of thirty hyenas. As the striped mass of zebras cantered off, barking, several of the trailing stallions paused again and again to attack the lead hyenas. One hyena suddenly was flung high over the zebras' backs. It landed, rolled over twice, and got up to continue running. Eventually the hyenas dropped back, a few at a time, and gave up.

WILD DOGS

These nomads of the African plains are the most highly social members of the dog family. They live in packs, each consisting of ten or eleven long-eared brownish dogs whose coats are splotched with white, black, and yellow. Pack formation increases their daytime hunting success and enables them to kill large prey, like zebras, that a single wild dog could not tackle. A leader (sometimes two or three) directs the pack's wide

roamings and selects the prey to be chased. Cooperation characterizes pack behavior. Both sexes hunt; the males share in the rearing of pups.

Early morning and late afternoon are hunting times. As the pack prepares for a hunt the wild dogs are exuberant. They dash about, colliding and leaping over backs, nuzzling each other and wagging their white-tipped tails. If there are pups in the pack one or more adults will stay behind when the pack sets off at a tireless trot, scanning the grassland for prey.

When a herd is spotted the pack closes ranks. Walking now, they continue their approach, in Schaller's words, "like a gang of street toughs before a fight." Zebras allow wild dogs to come close before they take evasive action. The pack may give short chase to several herds before finding a foal or sick zebra. Once a vulnerable animal is selected, the wild dogs' tails go up and they dash at the herd. The zebras canter off as braying barks and excited yips fill the air. Running beside the zebras as well as in front of them, the wild dogs dart in and out in an effort to scatter the group.

When the zebras scatter, the wild dogs close in. A zebra mare is grabbed and slowed to a stop. The chase is over. The mare stands motionless as one dog seizes her nose and others rip at her belly. Probably she is in shock. She puts up no fight as she is literally torn apart and eaten. Viscera are first to be consumed, then the wild dogs begin bolting down muscle meat. They chitter as they crowd around the kill, but there is no growling, snarling, or fighting. In fact, wild dogs are altruistic by nature. Not only do they share their food, but if pups are old enough to have followed along on short legs, the older animals back off to give them a chance to feed. Otherwise the adults gorge, and on their return to the den, regurgitate fresh meat for the pups. In less than an hour skin and skeleton are all that remain of the wild dogs' kill.

While studying wild dogs in the Serengeti, Dutch photographer Hugo van Lawick witnessed an unusual instance of zebra behavior when a mare and her two foals, one a suckling the other a yearling, were surrounded by a pack. The mare fought back with bared teeth and the yearling lunged forward when the dogs attempted to grab the foal. Suddenly the rest of the family group galloped to the rescue. The zebras bunched around the mare and her two offspring, wheeled, and galloped off in a tight formation that discouraged the wild dogs after a short chase.

Another curious incident is related by Cullen. A lone zebra, whose companions were some eighty-three elands, apparently gave courage to the large antelopes. The elands watched the zebra's aggressive rushes at a wild-dog pack, then lowered their spirally twisted, keeled horns, and joined the counterattack.

In spite of their large litters (as many as sixteen pups) wild dogs are rare animals. Probably their numbers are limited by outbreaks of distemper. Otherwise these canine coursers would rival lions and hyenas as important zebra predators.

CHEETAH

The cheetah is built for speed, with trim waist, deep chest, long slender legs, and small head. Because of its light body and relatively weak jaws, this solitary, fast-sprinting courser that hunts by day rarely attacks zebras. Its hunting is restricted to smaller prey species. On rare occasions a cheetah kills a zebra foal or a wildebeest calf. And, as there are always exceptions in the natural world, here are two recorded by Cullen: "Two

cheetah were seen on a half-grown zebra they had killed on the Kampi-ya-Mawe plains" (Tanzania Parks archives, 1963). "A group of four cheetah—all males—killed an adult zebra" (Kenya Parks archives, 1965).

LEOPARD

This secretive solitary spotted cat inhabits riverine forests that wind into the plains. It too preys on smaller animals such as gazelles, reedbucks,

baboons, jackals, and hyraxes. Usually it wedges its kill in a tree-branch larder. When zebra herds visit water holes within a leopard's territory there is always a chance that a foal will be ambushed.

SCAVENGERS

Scavengers congregate wherever a kill is made. Vultures are daytime scavengers; jackals are primarily nighttime scavengers, but often they are about by day as well. Rank is always observed at kills. Hyenas, of course, come first. Then jackals take their turns.

Vultures descend. Each species has its own feeding interest in the carcass. Large, heavy-beaked lappet-faced vultures and Ruppell's griffons threaten for position with their necks stretched and wings partly spread. Soon there is a melee of avian undertakers. Last to arrive at a carcass are the small, slender-beaked hooded and Egyptian vultures. Often marabou storks, ravens, kites, or a tawny eagle join the feeding vultures.

MAN

Man is the most deadly of all predators. On a small scale his poaching, the illegal hunting of protected wildlife, has little effect on animal populations. When prompted by commercialism instead of hunger, poaching becomes a nighttime activity, sometimes involving four-wheel-drive vehicles, high-velocity rifles, shotguns, and big trucks. All too often it results in wholesale slaughter of herd animals for their decorative hides and fly-whisk tails. It is a cruel and wasteful practice, but one with high profits. Until the demand for items made from skins is quelled in other countries there is little hope that poaching activities can be controlled in Africa's parks and game reserves.

Bows and arrows and spears are among the poacher's tools. A poison, derived by boiling bark and leaves of certain kinds of *Akokanthera* trees until a tarlike substance forms, is smeared on shaft and head of arrow or spear. The poachers hide by a water hole or along a well-used game trail.

When an arrow finds its mark in a zebra, death from disruption of heart-muscle contractions comes in less than an hour. The cruelest devices, however, are poachers' snares, 6-foot lengths of steel wire or plaited sisal which are placed along game trails and in riverine thicket

openings. When caught in a snare a zebra may struggle for hours or even days before it dies from loss of blood or exhaustion.

Once part of the balanced African-plains community, man was held in check by disease and tribal warfare. Nomadic cattle-herding tribes discouraged the spread of agricultural peoples into the grasslands. Today ever-increasing numbers of agriculturalists, with their spreading cultivation, and pastoralists, with their herds of cattle, goats, and sheep, lay claim to more and more of the plains and wooded grasslands. This destruction of habitat is the most serious of all threats to zebras and other wild grazers. For, as Norman Myers has written, "the hoe is stronger than the spear, and fencing wire is worse than the poacher's noose."

18. The Quagga— an Extinct Zebra

REDDISH-BROWN and striped only on its head, neck, and forequarters, the quagga (*Equus quagga*) was slightly taller and somewhat stockier than the plains zebra. Its dark brown stripes faded out behind the shoulders, or persisted as mottlings. An erect mane, alternately banded brown and white, topped its well-arched neck; a dark spinal stripe widened over its croup; its legs, undersides, and long, flowing tail were white. Although it was the most ponylike of all the zebras, the quagga was called *wilde esel* or wild ass by the early Cape colonists. The name quagga comes from the animal's barking call *qua-ha*, from which its Hottentot name *khoua-khoua* and its Afrikaans name *kwacha* are derived.

The quagga appears only briefly in recorded natural history. The 1758 edition of *Gleanings of Natural History* by George Edwards, naturalist and librarian in the Royal College of Surgeons, contains a stone lithograph mistakenly labeled as the female of the mountain zebra. Wrote Edwards: "This curious animal was brought alive, together with the male, from the Cape of Good Hope: the male dying before they arrived at London, I did not see it; but this female lived several years at a house of his Royal Highness the Prince of Wales, at Kew." The quagga's mistaken identity persisted until 1786 when Sparrman encountered herds of the partly striped chestnut-brown animals and assured the scientific world that quaggas came in both sexes.

Those fortunate enough to see the quagga generally agreed it was the most handsome of the zebras. Its mane, wrote the British artist Samuel Daniell in 1804, is "curious, appearing as if trimmed by art." Cornwallis Harris extolled quaggas for their "gay, glittering coats" that "sparkled like mica."

Some mammalogists, most of them German, regard the quagga as

a subspecies of the plains zebras (which they designate *Equus quagga* instead of *Equus burchelli*) and the southernmost extreme in the trend toward reduced leg banding and body striping. Other scientists maintain that the quagga is a distinct species which differs in skeletal characters as well as in color and stripe pattern. Large herds of quaggas and small groups of true Burchell's zebras once shared the same veld habitat, but their herds did not mingle and, as far as is known, interbreeding did not occur. This would seem evidence enough to regard the quagga as a distinct species.

Variation in color and extent of striping convinced Daniell that there were a number of different quaggas: "They are variously marked; some with waved stripes on the neck only, others with bands across the shoulder, other marked on the haunches, somewhat like the zebra." In 1909 British naturalist William Ridgeway listed fourteen quagga specimens in museums of Europe, South Africa, and Britain, with quaggas illustrated by Edwards, Daniell, Cornwallis Harris, and Lord Morton's quagga from a drawing by the noted French animal artist Jacques-

Laurent Agasse. Professor Ridgeway concluded that the variation among quaggas was due to environment and cautioned against haste in naming subspecies.

When quaggas roamed the karoos (dry tablelands) of the Cape Province and the plains of the Orange Free State south of the Vaal River in South Africa, they were, according to Cornwallis Harris, "sociable and peaceable, living carelessly, but sometimes in troops not exceeding twenty or thirty, but often in much larger communities. . . ." A long file of quaggas moving across "the profile of the ocean-like horizon" reminded him of "a rival caravan on its march." And he noted their tendency to range with the "white-tailed Gnoo and with the Ostrich." Hartebeests, sassabies, and bonteboks also were their grazing companions. In summer, when the veld was flower covered, the scattered quagga herds appeared "like fishing fleets on a multicolored sea." Scattered over the veld are polished rubbing rocks that are the quaggas' memorials.

When Burchell took part in a Boer quagga hunt in 1811 he reported "the whole plain seemed alive and appeared checquered black and white with their congregated masses." So astounding was the clatter of their hoofs that he likened the sound to "the din of a tremendous charge of cavalry." The galloping quaggas sent up clouds of dust and stones flew up from their heels, imperiling both eyes and teeth of their pursuers on horseback. Cornwallis Harris observed in 1840 that "nothing is easier than to turn the flank of the troop, which then immediately sounds the halt, and fronting the pursuer, gazes for a few seconds with distended nostrils."

For forty years Boer farmers and trekkers mercilessly slaughtered quaggas. Their guns could be heard booming in the distance day after day. Quagga hides were used to make sacks to carry dried peaches, quinces, walnuts, and grain. The thickened skin of the hock region was made into soles for homemade shoes the Boers called velschoons. Quagga meat, according to Burchell "between beef and mutton" in taste, was used to feed Hottentot servants. As the Dutch colonists prospered, farming spread inland and between 1850 and 1870 the slaughter of quagga herds was relentless.

Occasionally wounded quaggas took revenge. One animal lashed out with its hoofs and fractured a hunter's skull. Another turned and with its long, yellow teeth stripped all the fingers from its tormentor's hand. A third quagga, driven to the edge of a precipice by a Boer farmer, turned and seized the man's leg, dragging him from his horse and tearing his foot off at the ankle. According to Charles Williams who related the gory incident in *Travellers in Africa,* "mortification ensued, and he died a few days afterward."

Perhaps the last person to see quaggas in the wild was J. B. Evans who sighted three near the Tigerberg in the eastern part of South Africa's Great Karoo in 1858. Extermination was complete when the last known wild quagga was shot near Kingwilliamstown in 1861. Claims of quagga herds still living, one of them as recent as 1940, have all proved to be sightings of heat-haze-distorted Hartmann's mountain zebras.

After 1861 a few quaggas survived in zoos in London (until 1872), Berlin (until 1875), and Amsterdam. With the death of the Amsterdam zoo's mare on August 12, 1883, the quagga became extinct. Had zoos in the nineteenth century been concerned, as zoos today are, with the breeding of endangered animals the tragedy of the quagga's extinction might have been averted.

Quaggas did well in captivity. One of the several quaggas in the London zoo, a mare, was exhibited for twenty-one years. Purchased in 1851 by the Zoological Society for its zoo in Regent's Park, she was the only quagga photographed in life. There are three photographs of this mare: two were taken in the summer of 1872 (just before her death) by Frederick York; an 1870 photograph is attributed to Frank Haes. For a time the mare had company. In 1858 Sir George Gray, governor of the Cape Colony, presented a quagga stallion to the Zoological Society. Unfortunately, "by breaking down some boarding," the stallion injured himself so badly he had to be destroyed. But the quagga mare lived on until 1872.

What happened to the quagga mare after her death was for many years a mystery. Although the skin was discarded, the skeleton was known to have been saved. According to Professor Ridgeway, a 1909 letter from London taxidermist Edward Gerrard Jr. to Reginald I. Pocock, superintendent of the London zoo, stated that the skeleton was in the

British Museum (Natural History). However, on examination the skeleton proved to be that of a stallion (later identified as the London zoo quagga destroyed in 1864). Ridgeway left the matter of the missing quagga skeleton with these words: "Most fortunate it was that York photographed the female Quagga in the Gardens, for although her skeleton may be preserved in some museum, all record of her external appearance would have been lost."

Not until 1952, when David P. Willoughby visited various museums around the world in the course of his research on horses and zebras, was the mystery of the missing quagga unraveled. In the osteology collection of Yale University's Peabody Museum of Natural History Willoughby found the skeleton (YPM 1623), as well as a letter to Professor Othniel C. Marsh, dated April 14, 1873, in which Gerrard offered twelve specimens for sale, among them an unmounted quagga

skeleton for the sum of ten pounds. Professor Marsh, then deeply in-volved in the study of horse evolution, purchased the quagga for the museum that had just been founded by his uncle, George Peabody.

The only other quagga specimen in this hemisphere, the skull of a nine-year-old stallion, was obtained for the Academy of Natural Sciences in Philadelphia by Edward Drinker Cope. Throughout their long and distinguished careers in vertebrate paleontology, professors Marsh and Cope were bitter rivals, each seeking to outdo the other in his collections. Apparently their collecting zeal included recently extinct as well as fossil animals.

Some twenty-two skins, thirteen skulls, and fourteen skeletons of quaggas have been listed in museums of Britain, Europe, and South Africa. Probably the best mounted quagga is to be seen in the Sencken-berg Museum in Frankfurt, Germany.

19. Efforts to Breed and Train Zebras

In the wild, zebra species do not interbreed. This is so in northern Kenya, where the ranges of Grévy's zebra and plains zebra overlap and the species often associate in mixed herds, and in the Kaokoveld of southern Africa, where mountain zebras and plains zebras graze together. It was also true when the quagga and the Burchell's race of plains zebra shared the same veld habitat.

When animals are isolated from their own kind, as is often the case in captivity, they may become imprinted with behavior patterns of other species. In this way crosses have occurred between almost all species of the closely related equids.

Hybrids are the offspring of genetically dissimilar parents. Each species (the largest natural animal group capable of interbreeding to produce fertile offspring) has its own count of chromosomes. These are the tiny, paired, threadlike bodies in every cell which carry the hereditary units called genes. Grévy's zebra has forty-six chromosomes; plains zebras have forty-four; and mountain zebras have thirty-two. The domestic horse's chromosome count is sixty-four.

When sex cells are formed, chromosome numbers are halved, to be doubled again when male and female sex cells unite. A zebra hybrid, the offspring of two equid species, thus has genetic material that is incompatible. The two sets of chromosomes it inherits cannot mix because of differences in number, as well as in size and shape. In almost all instances zebra hybrids are sterile.

In captivity plains zebras have been crossed with mountain zebras. The foals produced have no dewlap and, except for larger ears and hindquarters stripe pattern, look more like the plains zebra parent. Attempts to breed a Grévy's zebra stallion to mountain zebra mares resulted in a high rate of abortion. A foal by a Somali wild ass out of a

116

mountain zebra mare was marked only by two transverse shoulder stripes, leg bands, and zebralike ear stripes. All three zebra species have been bred successfully with domestic horses. In fact, a Chapman's zebra stallion, kept by Friedrich von Falz-Fein at his Askania-Nova sanctuary-estate in southern Russia, preferred domestic mares to the zebra mare of his own kind. Eventually he turned on his mate and bit her to death.

Raymond Hook of Nanyuki, Kenya, bred the first zebroids by crossing a Grévy's zebra stallion with domestic mares. These hybrids have their sire's narrow stripes and tufted tail, but are more horselike in conformation and color. Strong, docile, and mulelike, sure-footed zebroids are used as pack animals by climbers on Mount Kenya's lower slopes. Foals also have come from Grévy's zebra-donkey mare crosses.

Crossbreeding experiments by the Hagenbecks, noted German animal dealers, produced zebrulas. Stripes are only faintly visible on these dark-bodied progeny of pony stallions and zebra mares. Other names for zebra hybrids include zebrule (zebra stallion-domestic mare), zebret (donkey stallion-zebra mare), and zebryde (zebra stallion-donkey mare).

One of the first attempts to tame zebras was made by the eighteenth-century French naturalist François LeVaillant, who claimed to have caught, saddled, and ridden a zebra without difficulty. In the late nineteenth century, Lord Lugard wrote of the possibilities of domesticating the zebra: "If this animal were tamed, the question of transport would be solved. Impervious to the tsetse fly, and to climatic diseases, it would be beyond calculation valuable."

Grévy's zebra generally was considered the most satisfactory species for domestication. In 1925 the photographer-sportsman Marius Maxwell wrote of a visit to Rattray's stable-boma on the track (road) to Archer's Post on the Uaso Nyiro River in northern Kenya, where he met Mr. Rattray, the "enterprising settler" engaged in capturing and breaking-in Grévy's zebras, and saw newly captured zebras. Maxwell photographed zebras in the boma, munching contentedly on what appear to be duom-palm leaves. Some have leather halters on. A mare in the foreground of Maxwell's picture has a cut and swollen right foreleg, presumably the result of capture struggles. Favorably impressed with Rattray's project and the good condition of his animals, Maxwell pointed out the important fact that, "in a country full of diseases for domestic animals," zebras possess natural immunity. Rattray himself claimed: "The Grévy is a much larger and more powerful animal, and is not so vicious as the Burchell [plains] zebra. Within a few weeks of capture I have inspanned them to pull well and steadily."

Quaggas too, were domesticated. In 1804 Daniell wrote: "They are tolerably swift; but the Boers sometimes succeed by stratagem to take them alive by throwing a noose of a rope over their heads. By domestication it soon becomes mild and tractable, and might be rendered useful by patient training; yet, abundant as they are . . . there are few instances of their being put to harness."

Sparrman, traveling through South Africa in 1775, described a quagga, captured as a foal, "so tame that it came to see us to be caressed." Like quaggas on many Boer farms, this one was kept as protection for horses and sheep. Added Sparrman: "It was said never to be frightened by the hyaena, but on the contrary . . . would pursue this

fierce animal . . . so that it was a most certain guard for the horses, with which it was turned out to grass at night."

In the Cape Colony and on the island of Mauritius quaggas occasionally were used as driving animals. An imported pair, harnessed to a phaeton and driven by its owner, Mr. Sheriff Parkins, caused a stir in London during the early nineteenth century. Noted the French naturalist Baron Georges Cuvier: "Among the equipages occasionally exhibited in the gay season in Hyde Park, and other fashionable places of resort, may be seen [one] drawn by two Couaggas, which seem as subservient to the curb and whip as any well-trained horses."

During the 1820s the Windsor Castle menagerie included a quagga. Somewhat later the London zoo's quaggas could be seen pulling the forage wagon between Regent's Park and the Covent Garden Market. Of all the zebras, horse authority Charles Hamilton Smith considered the quagga as "unquestionably the best calculated for domestication both as regards strength and docility." He claimed to have driven a quagga that showed "as much temper and delicacy of mouth as any domestic horse."

The fang-stock, a stout 5-foot pole, was used to capture Burchell's zebras. Galloping alongside, the rider dropped a running noose over the zebra's head. Once caught, the zebra's fight was short and, according to Millais, "after being tied up to a post in camp for a week, they often require no further taming . . . becoming almost too friendly." The Honorable Walter Rothschild, of the British banking family, purchased three Burchell's zebras and had them trained. His zebras, driven singly and as a pair, became a familiar sight on the London streets.

Plains zebras also were domesticated, although as A. Blayney Percival noted, they were less hardy than Grévy's zebra and often died from exhaustion when captured. However, Sir Richard Lyddeker reported: "They respond quickly to the whip when pulling, they are not given to plunging, but crouch down and pull steadily; they keep their condition without corn-feeding, and they appear more intelligent than mules or donkeys."

Zebra farms were established during the late nineteenth century, among them the Baron von Schellendorf's at Mbuguni, southeast of Mount Kilimanjaro. For a time a herd was kept on a government farm

near Naivasha in Kenya. Ten pounds and upward was the going price for a plains zebra.

A photograph exists of a plains zebra four-in-hand pulling a two-wheeled Cape cart. More often plains zebras were inspanned with mules. Presumably the mules exerted a steadying influence on their wild relatives. During the late nineteenth century the Messrs. Zeedesberg, coach contractors of Petersberg in the Transvaal district of South Africa, used plains zebras in harness. Four of their eight Chapman's zebras, all captured by hunter's lasso, were quiet enough to be inspanned with three mules and a donkey behind a lead pair of mules and used to pull one of the company's four-wheeled coaches. This hitch is depicted, stopped in front of the Transvaal Hotel in Petersberg, in *Horses, Asses, Zebras, and Mules*, written in 1895 by W. B. Tegetmeier and C. L. Sutherland. A Mr. Harold Stephens is quoted on the zebras: "They pull well and are very willing, and never jib . . . when inspanned [they] stand quite still and wait for the word to go, they pull up when required, and are perfectly amenable to the bridle . . . they never kick [but] when first handled . . . have an inclination to bite." Mr. Zeedesberg himself hoped to replace his mules with zebras "as the zebra is free from that scourge of South Africa commonly called 'horse sickness,' which . . . costs an enormous amount to coach proprietors in horse flesh during the summer season."

Another hitch that included two oxen, two elands, two plains zebras, and two mules belonged to Carl Hagenbeck and was driven within the confines of his Hamburg menagerie.

Captain M. H. Hayes, a well-known horseman in his time, regarded the plains zebra as a "very easy animal to tame." At an 1892 agricultural show in Pretoria, South Africa, he claimed to have broken in a plains zebra "without having to throw him down, tie him head to tail, or to resort to any of the other heroic methods of the horse-tamer." After a half-hour of handling, this zebra was quiet enough to be ridden.

Captain Hayes was less enthusiastic about the mountain zebra, an animal he considered extremely difficult to subdue. Small size, short neck, straight shoulder, long lower-leg bones and donkeylike conformation combine to make the mountain zebra the least suited for "civilized requirement." Hamilton Smith, also a horseman, termed the mountain zebra generally "vicious and fierce," but noted that a mare in a Paris menagerie was gentle enough for riding. The most celebrated mountain zebra under saddle was an aged stallion that belonged to a traveling menagerie in India. In two days Captain Hayes broke this zebra to saddle. Apparently he had sufficient trust in the stallion and his own training methods to allow Mrs. Hayes, in elegant sidesaddle attire, to mount long enough to be photographed.

Of all attempts to domesticate zebras, the American explorer-sculptor Carl Akeley wrote: "this is done only for the amusement it affords, because the zebra, like all wild animals, has never quite enough of the endurance that is bred into a domesticated horse to make him useful in harness . . . he requires only sufficient stamina to outrun a lion for a short distance." In fact, zebras in zoos generally are considered intractable. Akeley himself, however, must have regarded zebras with some affection. In spite of the many collecting expeditions he led for various museums, he admitted to being "particularly thin-skinned when it came to shooting" these animals that reminded him of "domesticated friends."

20. Zebras in Captivity

ACCORDING to Lee S. Crandall, for many years a curator at the New York Zoological Park, zebras require a heated stable during winter and daily turnout when weather permits. Lamenting the public's obsession with feeding animals, Crandall noted that the 7-foot-high zebra enclosures were covered with 2-inch wire mesh to guard against the animal's biting tidbit-ladden fingers.

Lack of activity and a too soft substrate lead to excessive growth of the hoofs, a common problem with zebras in captivity. When their hoofs must be cut back or pared, zebras usually have to be tranquilized, always a difficult and risky procedure. Most zoos use a mixture of asphalt and crushed stone that provides good resilient footing and prevents excessive hoof growth.

Zebra diets are similar to horses': hay (as much as 20 pounds a day), 3 or 4 quarts of crushed oats, with treats of carrots, apples, and potatoes, and water to drink and a salt block to lick.

Zoos sometimes exhibit plains zebras with other animals in spacious African plains scenes. Grévy's zebras, however, are prone to attack and kill impalas and other antelopes, even when they share a zoo habitat as large as 70 acres.

The artist Paul Bransom, who in the early years of this century enjoyed a studio of his own in the Lion House at the Bronx zoo, told of a Grévy's zebra stallion whose temperament made him feared by his keepers. One winter day, when there were few visitors in the zoo, a keeper effigy was set up in the zebra's paddock. As keepers, curators, and Mr. Bransom looked on, the stallion was turned out. Slowly, stealthily he made his way along the fence, eyeing the "keeper." Suddenly, and with apparent savage intent, he lunged at the effigy, toppling it and causing its cabbage head to roll off some distance. Angrily the zebra stomped with his forefeet on the body of the "keeper." Then, his fury spent, he turned and began munching on the cabbage that had been the "keeper's" head.

Possibly the first zebra to be foaled in captivity in this country was a filly born in New Rochelle, New York. George N. Wilson of the Westchester County Historical Society supplied this account from the *New Rochelle Pioneer* of May 26, 1900: "A young zebra was born in the Glen Island Zoo early Thursday morning . . . the first animal of its kind ever born in captivity. . . . The young zebra has black and white stripes around the entire body and is said to be the finest marked animal in the country. It is valued at $2,000."

Zebras breed well in captivity and tend to be long-lived. A Chapman's zebra mare in the Basel zoo lived for twenty-eight years, while a Grévy's zebra mare acquired by the New York Zoological Park as a two-year-old in 1947 lived in the zoo until her death in 1975. Twenty-eight and thirty years are long life spans for any of the equids.

GLOSSARY

SUGGESTIONS FOR FURTHER READING

INDEX

Glossary

brachydont: a term used to describe teeth with low crowns and well-developed roots; the tooth condition in early browsing horses and in man

cannon bone: the enlarged metapodial (metacarpal or metatarsal) of the third digit, supporting the equid leg from knee or hock to fetlock joint

check ligaments: fibrous bands, two in the foreleg and one in the hindleg, that supplement the action of the flexor muscles and reduce the strain of standing

chestnuts: flattened oval horny structures, one on the inside of each zebra foreleg above the knee

coffin bone: the expanded terminal segment (Phalanx III) that carries the hoof

countershading: a form of natural deception which causes loss of the normal visual clues by means of which an animal is recognizable

croup: point of rump

dewlap: fold of pendant skin on underside of neck; a mountain zebra characteristic

diastema: a gap between teeth in a jaw; in equids between incisors and cheek teeth

ergot: the wartlike spur on the back of each fetlock joint

fetlock joint: the joint of an equid limb between cannon bone and the larger pastern bone

Flehmen: the grimace in which upper lip is curled and head is raised; usually connected with mating activities

flehming: the assessing of an odor; zebra stallions commonly flehm the urine of mares

frog: the horny elastic V-shaped pad on the underside of an equid's hoof

gridiron pattern: a mountain zebra characteristic, this pattern is formed by a series of short transverse stripes that connect spinal stripe and uppermost rump stripes

hand: a unit of measurement used to express the height of an equid at the withers; a hand equals 4 inches

hock: an equid's ankle or tarsus

hypsodont: a term used to describe teeth that have high crowns and short roots; the typical tooth condition of grazers

infundibula: small cup-shaped depressions on the biting surface of equid incisors

lophodont: a term used to describe cheek teeth with crests or ridges on their grinding surface

mesaxonic: having the axis of the foot formed by the middle, or third, digit

molariform: molarlike

navicular: a shuttle-shaped sesamoid bone, suspended in the deep flexor tendon and located behind the coffin bone

optical disruption: the breaking up of form and outline; achieved in zebras by stripe direction

127

panniculus adiposus: the layer of fat that usually pads a zebra's body

pastern: the sloping portion of an equid limb between fetlock joint and hoof, formed by first and second segments (Phalanges I and II) of the third digit

perissodactyls: odd-toed hoofed mammals belonging to the order Perissodactyla

preorbital pit: a depression in front of the orbit or eye socket

Rossigkeitgesicht: A descriptive term (from the German) for the open-mouth, ears-back, submissive facial expression of an estrous mare

sesamoids: two small bones at the back of the fetlock joint

shadow stripes: the somewhat less distinct stripes that mark the interspaces on hindquarters and flanks of some zebras

splint bones: the much-reduced remnants of an equid's lateral metapodials

stay apparatus: a system of opposing tendons and ligaments which counterbalance in the standing equid limb

stifle: the true knee, or patella, of an equid

withers: point of shoulders

wolf teeth: an equid's peglike deciduous premolars, usually not replaced in the permanent dentition

Suggestions for Further Reading

Estes, Richard D. "Trials of a Zebra Herd Stallion," *Natural History* 76 (1967), 58–65.
———. "Zebras Offer Clues to the Way Wild Horses Once Lived," *Smithsonian* 5 (1974), 100–107.
Fletcher, Colin. *The Winds of Mara.* New York: Alfred A. Knopf, 1973.
Groves, Colin P. *Horses, Asses and Zebras in the Wild.* Hollywood, Fla.: Ralph Curtis Books, 1974.
Grzimek, Bernhard and Michael. *Serengeti Shall Not Die.* New York: E. P. Dutton, 1961.
Klingel, Hans. "Social Behaviour of African Equidae," *Zoologica Africana* 7 (1972), 175–85.
Mochi, Ugo, and Carter, T. Donald. *Hoofed Mammals of the World.* New York: Charles Scribner's Sons, 1953; reissued 1971.
Myers, Norman. *The Long African Day.* New York: Macmillan Publishing Co., 1972.
Schaller, George B. *Golden Shadows, Flying Hooves.* New York: Alfred A. Knopf, 1973.
Simpson, George Gaylord. *Horses.* New York: Oxford University Press, 1951.
van Lawick-Goodall, Hugo and Jane. *Innocent Killers.* Boston: Houghton Mifflin Co., 1971.
Willoughby, David P. *The Empire of Equus.* South Brunswick and New York: A. S. Barnes & Co., 1974.

Index

Agasse, Jacques-Laurent, 112
Akeley, Carl, 121-122
alarm calls, 25-26
albinism, 33-34
Amboseli National Park (Kenya), 75
anthrax, 92
Astley Maberly, Charles T., 95

bachelor bands, 42, 58, 72, 89, 101; colts joining, 57; home range, 88; older stallions, 56-57
Backhaus, Dieter, 53
barking, 25, 101-102
Bell, Richard H. V., 72
biting, 62-63, 83, 93, 95; in captivity, 121, 123
bloodworms (strongyles), 91
Böhm's zebra (Equus burchelli boehmi), 46-47, 86-88. See also Grant's zebra
bonds: family group, 54, 56, 58, 78; father-son, 56; mare-foal, 67, 69-70; between stallions, 58
botflies, 91
Bransom, Paul, 123
broken limbs, 93
Buffon, Georges Louis Leclerc, Comte de, 27
bunching, 54, 95
Burchell, William J., 41-42, 49, 112
Burchell's zebra (Equus burchelli burchelli), 45, 48-50, 110, 119

Cabrera, Angel, 45
Camp, Charles L., 17
Cape mountain zebra (Equus zebra zebra), 40-43, 51
Caracalla (Marcus Aurelius Antoninus), 35
cattle egrets, 77
chalicotheres, 8
Chapman's zebra (Equus burchelli antiquorum), 47-49, 117, 124. See also Damaraland zebra
check ligaments, 85
cheetah, 95, 103-104
chestnuts, 21
circuses, 35-37, 45, 124
communication, 55
concealing coloration, 29-31
condylarths, 10

Cope, Edward Drinker, 115
countershading, 31
Crandall, Lee S., 123
croup, 17, 80
crowned crane, 77
Cullen, Anthony, 66, 103
Cuvier, Georges, 119

Damaraland zebra (Equus burchelli antiquorum), 47-49, 90. See also Chapman's zebra
Daniell, Samuel, 109, 110, 112, 118
defense (by family stallions): against other stallions, 56; against predators, 54, 66, 81, 95, 100-101
dewlap, 40, 116
diet, 72-73, 123
diseases, 92-93, 117, 121
Dolichohippus, 38
dominance, 55-56, 58
drinking, 58, 60, 81
dung piles, 59, 60

ears, 19, 75, 94; in communication, 55; Grévy's zebra, 38; hybrids, 116
Edwards, George, 109, 112
elands, 103
eohippus (Hyracotherium), 10 11, 59
Equidae, 5, 8
equids: fossil, 10-13; living, 5-9
Equus, 5, 12-13
Equus occidentalis, 13
ergot, 21
erythrism, 33
Estes, Richard D., 26, 53, 63, 78
estrus, 57, 61-62, 64
Etosha National Park (South West Africa), 43, 51, 53, 66
Evans, J. B., 113
eyes, 14, 18, 75, 94

facial stripes, 33, 38
family groups, 54-55; home range, 88; mares, 56; mountain zebras, 42, 90; plains zebras, 54-57, 62, 89; security in, 68, 95, 100-101, 103
fencing, 44, 108